Navigating PDA in America

NAVIGATING
PDA
IN AMERICA

A Framework to Support Anxious, Demand-Avoidant
Autistic Children, Teens and Young Adults

Ruth Fidler and Diane Gould

Foreword by Sarah C. Wayland, Ph.D.

Jessica Kingsley Publishers
London and Philadelphia

First published in Great Britain in 2024 by Jessica Kingsley Publishers
An imprint of John Murray Press

1

A CIP catalogue record for this title is available from the
British Library and the Library of Congress

ISBN 978 1 83997 274 4
eISBN 978 1 83997 273 7

Printed and bound in the United States by Integrated Books International

Jessica Kingsley Publishers' policy is to use papers that are natural, renewable and recyclable products and made from wood grown in sustainable forests. The logging and manufacturing processes are expected to conform to the environmental regulations of the country of origin.

Jessica Kingsley Publishers
Carmelite House
50 Victoria Embankment
London EC4Y 0DZ

www.jkp.com

John Murray Press
Part of Hodder & Stoughton Limited
An Hachette UK Company

Contents

Contents

Foreword

This book is profoundly important. It will help caregivers, educators and clinicians understand a group of children who have heretofore been grossly misunderstood—those with PDA. Not only will readers finally get a clear description of the PDA profile, they will also learn why PDAers struggle. Most importantly, adults supporting kids with PDA will find a comprehensive framework that will help them think about how to support the emotional wellbeing of PDAers, while also making it possible for them to learn and grow—at home, and at school.

Why do I love this book so much? Because if it had been available 15 years ago, when I needed it, it would have helped our family.

In October of 2006, my four-year-old son was in his fourth childcare placement, on the verge of being asked to leave. No one could figure him out. I dreaded the daily pickup routine; the "airing of grievances" made my heart ache for my sweet sensitive son, who couldn't understand why the other children and the adults wouldn't just do as he asked.

When we asked for a diagnostic review from a developmental pediatrician, he hesitated to diagnose autism. He was concerned that it didn't fit because our son was adept at using social strategies to distract us and desperately wanted to play with the other kids. After a long discussion, he decided that autism was the most accurate description of our son's profile; this allowed us to get insurance reimbursement for therapies and supports from the school system.

How we wished for a clear diagnosis and a straightforward explanation of what my son found difficult.

A few years later, I came across an article describing a group of children with "Pathological Demand Avoidance" (PDA) who had unpredictably strong emotions and obsessively resisted demands.

As I read the paper, I was struck by how closely my son fit the profile. In addition to mood lability and extreme panic attacks, he was extremely attached to me (and *only* me in those early years), seemed oblivious to social hierarchies, resisted speech-language therapy with all his might, and charmed strangers with his enthusiasm and engaging monologues. Getting him to do anything was nearly impossible. He fired me and my husband on more than one occasion for making unacceptable demands. Truth be told, my husband and I had mostly given up on any but the most critically important requests.

Was it possible that understanding PDA could help us figure out what he needed?

We had tried all the usual strategies, including clear rules, routines and consistency. They didn't help, and we often felt like they were just one more thing to fight about. The stickers and stars of reward systems weren't any help either. For a long time, I blamed myself, thinking I wasn't consistent enough, but years later my son observed that those systems offended him because they were "treating me like a dog!" The only approach that truly worked was collaborating with him.

Likewise, it was critical for our son's wellbeing to validate his feelings. I vividly remember the first time I empathized without trying to educate or solve the problem. A simple "That must have been really hard!" was like magic. He needed to know that we could see his pain and understood that it was difficult for him. We also found that he really connected with teachers who had a good sense of humor, were patient and innovative, and, most of all, flexible.

I wish we had known from the start how important it was to focus on his emotional wellbeing, rather than his behavior, both at home and at school.

In 2013, I started a business dedicated to helping other parents learn to support their unique and creative children in a professional capacity. The parents were scared, exhausted and—worst of all—they felt judged.

How I wanted a guide to help these parents feel less alone. I wanted them to know that their experiences were not isolated or unique. I also wished for a framework to help them determine the best ways to understand and support their children.

Now, today, because of the hard work of Diane Gould at PDA North America, people with PDA profiles and their loved ones living in the United States can get support, guidance, and understanding. PDA is slowly gaining recognition, and with it, those with PDA and their loved ones have access to a community who understands them.

With this book, my wishes have been answered! Ruth Fidler and Diane Gould have partnered to provide, in one place, the wisdom I desperately wanted. The quotes from caregivers, educators and PDA individuals give voice to their experiences, providing a powerful perspective. Readers will learn about the PDA profile and gain a deeper understanding of PDAers' struggles, along with strategies for supporting and understanding emotional wellbeing, so the PDA person they love can move forward and grow.

The insight, understanding and wisdom in this book will inspire you to approach PDA individuals and their families with curiosity and compassion. All you have to do is read on!

Sarah C. Wayland, Ph.D.
Founder, Guiding Exceptional Parents
Co-author, *Is This Autism? A Guide for Clinicians and Everyone Else*

INTRODUCTION

This book is mainly intended for professionals and families who support a child, teenager or young adult with a pathological demand avoidant (PDA) profile. It outlines our current understanding of PDA and associated approaches that, in our experience, are effective in positively supporting PDA individuals to thrive and to learn.

As our understanding of autism and of PDA develops, it is important that we continue to deepen our knowledge. We are a long way from knowing all the answers, so it is also important that we step outside our echo chambers when we share our own views as well as when we listen to those which may differ from our own.

Conceptions of PDA are at the early stages in America. As awareness of autism is developing to include less common and more complex presentations of autism, it is hoped that recognition of PDA will be incorporated into this broadening outlook. Currently, PDA individuals living in America are not likely to have received a diagnosis, not because they are not there, but because recognition and assessment are not yet aligned with their profile. Some of them may have no diagnosis, others may have received an alternative diagnosis which may or may not be a helpful one.

Perspectives of a variety of people are included in this book. There are contributions from PDA children, teenagers and young adults, from their parents (some of whom may be autistic themselves), from healthcare professionals and from educators. Many, but not all, of these contributors are neurodivergent and each perspective brings its own experience; all, therefore, are of value.

There are a number of different terms in current use regarding how we refer to individuals and use of language is evolving quickly. In order to reflect the varying preferences and practices of different groups we will use both person-first language when talking about a person with a PDA profile or a person with autism, and also refer to individuals as autistic, PDA individuals or the more informal term PDAer. We intend this approach to be respectful and inclusive, and to remind all readers that there are different preferences across communities. No one group can speak for everyone. If you are supporting an individual, we suggest it is best not to make assumptions, and to talk to them about which terminology they are most comfortable with.

We use the term "PDA" throughout. There are ongoing debates about our notions of PDA and associated terminology, but we continue to use it for a number of reasons:

- It is the original term coined by Professor Elizabeth Newson, who first identified this profile.
- It is the term that is gaining traction and international recognition.
- It is helpful to have a conceptualization to refer to that describes an individual's profile holistically, rather than to list associated traits.
- It is a term that will currently lead interested people to the appropriate resources.
- It is the term widely used in research studies and publications.
- It highlights that the anxiety-driven avoidance in PDA is outside the range of ordinary behavior in a way that is beyond the deliberate choice of the PDAer, because it is intrinsic to their profile.

Some prefer other terminology. Whatever is used in the future, it is crucial that the core representation continues to clarify that avoiding demands or having a drive for autonomy is not as a result of individuals being deliberately difficult, confrontational or controlling, but is an integral part of a person's neurology, sensitivities and presentation of their autism.

Our position regarding PDA is that it is best understood as an autism profile. Autism is dimensional in nature, so not only will each individual have their own profile, but some people will also have other co-existing conditions which overlap and interlock, impacting individuals in different ways. This means that although we can outline key principles there is not one single route to support. This book offers suggested components of a support package. How you create your own combination of them is as individual as the child or young person you know, and will depend on the detailed collaboration of the team around them. Indeed, flexible, personalized, creative and sensitive approaches are at the heart of what we recommend for all supporting adults, whatever their role.

There are a number of autistic children and young people who experience high anxiety. Demand avoidance can be a response to their anxiety but this does not mean that all demand-avoidant autistic people necessarily have a PDA profile. Understanding a PDA profile is about understanding its basis within the autism spectrum alongside its core characteristics. Furthermore, the approaches outlined here are not exclusive to children with a PDA profile, so there may be some strategies that will benefit others, whether diagnosed or not, whether attending school settings or not.

We refer to PDA individuals as she, he or they, depending on the context, though we recognize that some individuals may have preferred pronouns. This use of language reflects the choices of the people concerned. Again, we suggest it is best to talk to individuals about their personal preferences.

It is important to acknowledge that the authors are not PDAers and have not parented children with a PDA profile, although they have other neurodivergent people in their families. However, over their careers they have supported hundreds, if not thousands, of young people, their families and the multidisciplinary professionals who work with them. Their experience has been developed over a combined 75-plus years of working in education and clinical services, contributing to assessments, providing consultation and training, as well as working directly with young people and their families.

There is a history in America of using behavioral approaches with autistic children. These approaches are not effective or recommended for individuals with a PDA profile because they are not sufficiently flexible and invariably contribute to further anxiety. The authors do not endorse using these approaches with PDAers.

Throughout the book we have used anonymized case studies and practical examples, based on our own experience as well as reports from families we have known, for which we are very grateful.

All pages marked with ★ can be downloaded from www.jkp.com/catalogue/book/9781839972744. Pages will be available to download as shown, with example text included, and will also be available as blank templates to utilize for personal use.

CHAPTER 1

UNDERSTANDING PDA

You are probably reading this book because you have encountered some concern and confusion regarding parenting or educating a young person you know. Most probably you will have already tried the usual recommended parenting and teaching approaches which may have worked well with other children in your care. But in this instance, they do not seem to be helping. In fact, they may even seem to be making things worse. So, you are now looking for an alternative way to connect because you have realized that to help them thrive, you need to understand this person in a different way.

Effective support for children with pathological demand avoidance (PDA) tends to succeed or fail on the basis of how well the child and the adult engage with each other, how positive and trusting the relationships are with supporting adults, and how flexible the approaches can be. We will explore various ways to achieve this, but first it's important to understand the nature of PDA so we can appreciate *why* these approaches are suitable. If we are to meet the needs of a young person, first we must understand what their needs are and what might be underlying their behavior. It is from that position of understanding and acceptance that we can then begin to plan.

It is not unusual to hear from parents like Ellen, who said:

Our son had an autism diagnosis when he was little but it never quite fitted. Evaluations often added words like "atypical" or "traits" but wouldn't mention PDA. It meant that the reports we were given left us in a wilderness, still guessing about how to support him.

There is an increasing awareness of PDA across various professional fields as well as internationally and, inevitably, some countries are further along the line than others for a whole host of reasons.

As authors, one of us is very familiar with the context of North America and the other with the UK. Our two countries are at different places in terms of recognition of PDA as a diagnostic formulation. Frankly, there is even variation within our own countries in terms of understanding of PDA, and we certainly work within very different systems. Our aim is not to compare, but to use our experience and knowledge to focus on practical ways to support youngsters with a PDA profile wherever they may live.

Although, as authors, we have different backgrounds, what we have in common is an understanding of the distinctive needs of the group of children, adolescents and young adults who match the PDA profile. We are both driven by wanting these children to be recognized in order to have their needs met. We want to lay out a framework for supporting families and professionals so they can develop an effective pathway for the children, adolescents and young adults they know. It is a pathway that is rooted in understanding an individual's personal profile; therefore it should be possible to implement with or without a formal diagnosis.

This book is primarily written for readers who are living in America and who are navigating the systems of education, health and family support available there. What we hope is that the framework can be adapted to whatever situation a family or education setting finds themselves in. It is recognized that America is at the relatively early stages of understanding and acknowledging PDA and the needs of PDAers, but what we are setting out here is an optimistic and forward-thinking model of support.

WHAT IS PDA?

Some readers may already have a lot of knowledge about PDA; for others this may be their first contact with it. Here we will explore the key characteristics of the PDA profile and start to build toward creating a picture of the impact of PDA on individuals.

"Pathological demand avoidance" is a term first used by Elizabeth Newson in the 1980s. She was working as a psychologist at the Child Development Research Centre at the University of Nottingham, UK. She had extensive experience in the field of autism and at the time was running an assessment clinic where she saw children who were referred from all over the UK. She began to see a number of children who were described as "reminiscent" of others with autism but who had some subtle yet significant differences. In time, she came to agree that the children she saw had different characteristics from other autistic children, although they did share many key features. Crucially, though, they were similar to each other. This was her "light-bulb" moment. The children shared what she described as "an obsessional avoidance of the ordinary demands of everyday life" (Newson, Le Maréchal & David 2003). It was at that point she felt she had identified a distinctive group (known then as the family of pervasive developmental disorders, PDD). She developed the conceptualization of PDA that is what we would now describe as a distinct profile of autism.

The first peer-reviewed paper on PDA was published in 2003 (Newson et al. 2003). In recent years there have been further research papers and more publications. They can be accessed via the PDA Society website (www.pdasociety.org.uk). Some emerging themes from research thus far include the following:

- PDA features can vary across the autism spectrum (O'Nions et al. 2016a).
- The PDA profile represents a constellation of behavioral characteristics.

- There is a more even gender distribution in PDA than in other autism profiles.
- PDA is comparatively rare across the autism spectrum.
- Although there are some parallels with behaviors arising from "disruptive behavior disorders," there are several important differences in the nature of the behaviors as well as in the strategies that are effective.

Further research is needed to explore issues such as types of demand avoidance; what represents triggers for some plus what approaches make demands more tolerable for others; and how understanding the cognitive and emotional processing profile of PDA individuals contributes toward greater consensus about how to best describe PDA.

Current research has generated debate about PDA, and there are differing views on diagnostic formulations. However, there is some agreement among professionals, who are seeing youngsters across a range of clinical services or education settings who are described by their families and their teachers with the same constellation of features. It is important that debate about the use of the diagnostic formulation does not distract from the real priority, which is ultimately about valuing difference and meeting the needs of the individuals with a PDA profile.

Our position is that PDA is a profile within the autism spectrum. That means, of course, that someone can't have a PDA profile without being autistic. Although PDA doesn't currently appear specifically in the diagnostic manuals, it is gaining recognition. According to the diagnostic manual (DSM-5-TR; American Psychiatric Association 2022), autism is characterized by difficulties with communication and social interaction alongside the presence, since early childhood, of repetitive behavior, inflexibility and restricted interests, and sensory differences that have a pervasive impact on everyday life. These are autistic characteristics that also underlie a PDA profile, meaning that some of the issues regarding resistance are likely to interlock with difficulties related to flexible thinking as well as raised anxiety; and that some of the difficulties regarding social understanding relate to areas of difference in social interaction as a core feature of autism.

Despite ongoing debate about the nature of PDA, when we recognize a child who has communication differences, who can become fixated on something or someone, who has sensory sensitivities, who struggles to tolerate uncertainty, and who finds it hard to predict social outcomes, it's hard to see how a child with those particular differences wouldn't be described as autistic. It is viewing PDA in this context that gives us a holistic understanding of a condition that best describes the cluster of features we see.

PDA is comparatively rare, if we look at the whole of the autism spectrum, affecting a small percentage of the total population. However, autism is more prevalent than previously thought. Figures published by the Centers for Disease Control and Prevention (CDC) for children of eight years old have increased from 1 in 150 in 2000 to 1 in 59 in 2014, to 1 in 54 in 2016, to 1 in 44 in 2018 and more recently to 1 in 36 in 2020 (Maenner et al. 2023).

Christopher Gillberg's population-based study (Gillberg et al. 2015) estimated that PDA features in autism spectrum conditions at a rate of 1 in 25, suggesting if we were to take 100 individuals with an autism spectrum condition, around four of them would have a PDA profile. This figure will benefit from more research as we move forward in our identification of PDA, especially in the light of the increased prevalence figures of autism.

Children and teenagers with a PDA profile can be particularly complex to support and to teach. Most school environments operate in anticipation of compliance on the part of pupils which, for those with a PDA profile, exacerbates the child's sense of losing autonomy. When this mismatch happens repeatedly it is not hard to see how school placements become precarious and potentially traumatic for some. Gore Langton and Frederickson (2016) describe pupils with a PDA profile who "were much more likely than children in the general population to have experienced all forms of exclusion from school... These findings are particularly striking given that the children were, on average, only half-way through their school careers."

Even thinking in terms such as "teaching" can present challenges to PDAers, because teaching implies delivering content along with expectations of completing work tasks, on which there may also be a test. Instead, it can be more useful to view the role of an educator as someone who "facilitates learning" rather than as someone who "dispenses teaching." A shift of emphasis like this shares control in the learning process and makes it a tandem endeavor.

The behavioral features of PDA, like other autistic profiles, are dimensional (O'Nions et al. 2016a). There will be overlapping strengths and challenges in PDAers that are unique to them. Individuals will be affected in different ways, although there are common themes underlying those differences. For parents and professionals, it is supportive to develop a personal profile of an individual so that there is a shared and holistic understanding of their needs.

There is ongoing discussion regarding the terminology around PDA, specifically the word "pathological." This is the term that was first used by Elizabeth Newson in the 1980s when the broader connotations associated with the word were different from today. Some people are beginning to use the word "extreme" instead of or alongside pathological. Alternatively they might refer to "autism with a demand-avoidant profile." We have some empathy with those who are uncomfortable with the use of the word "pathological." We certainly do not mean to pathologize the condition, but PDA is the term that is gaining recognition, so, for the sake of deepening our understanding of the profile, that is the terminology we use. It does not need to get in the way of us celebrating difference and valuing autistic individuals. Among reasons to use the PDA terminology are those listed in the Introduction. It is also interesting to note the rationale of Elizabeth Newson in selecting the word "pathological."

She was referring to children whose behavior was outside the range of ordinary to a clinically significant extent. She was trying to clarify that the children could not help their responses, and that these responses had a significant impact on their day-to-day functioning. It is this context of the condition being described as "pathological" that she intended. The PDA Society comment that "Professor Newson herself later expressed regret over her use of the term. Many individuals who identify with the profile feel that the term is accurate and appropriate, as the demand avoidance they experience is innate and all-consuming" (PDA Society 2022).

While we recognize this debate, which no doubt will be ongoing, what matters most is understanding the needs of the children and their families. As O'Nions et al. (2016b) state:

> At present, there is considerable controversy about the usefulness of the term pathological demand avoidance, which is distracting from the real imperative... Appropriate description and formulation of the child's difficulties is the starting point for the identification of potential management strategies and appropriate educational support. It is essential that this help is provided to these very vulnerable individuals and their families.

THE KEY CHARACTERISTICS OF A PDA PROFILE

The key characteristics are set out here but, remembering that they are dimensional, we need to keep an individual's personal profile at the heart of any input. It can be helpful to view the features of PDA as ingredients in a recipe, used in varying proportions, made by different chefs, so we should not expect every dish to turn out the same! Elizabeth Newson herself used to describe a diagnosis as a way to "make sense" of a person. When we can understand what makes sense *of* a person and what makes sense *to* a person, then we can start to support them effectively. Moreover, we should keep in mind that people change as they mature and develop, so the eight-year-old PDA child may present with different strengths and challenges to how they are by age 18 or 28.

Resists and avoids the ordinary demands of everyday life

Lots of children don't really want to do what the adults around them would prefer that they did. In fact, many of us at any age sometimes don't want to do what is being asked of us. There may be all sorts of understandable reasons, some of which demonstrate that we are actually making reasonable choices, or simply reflect that we are emotional creatures and our moods fluctuate on different days depending on the situation and on who is asking us to do something. That is not out of the ordinary. What we are talking about in PDA is avoidance with increased frequency, intensity and impact on daily lives and relationships. For those of you who are accustomed to spending time with a PDAer, this extreme avoidance is probably the one characteristic that stands out the most. It may be the most notable, but is not the only trait.

When we look at the quality of the avoidance, we see features that are characteristic of PDA. It's not just about avoiding the events that most children resist because they are anxious, such as starting school, or the tasks that leave most children uninspired, such as tidying their bedrooms or learning words for a spelling test. We see children who will resist and avoid the mundane, ordinary expectations of everyday life, including requests that they may usually be capable of complying with and those we have reason to think they would usually enjoy. There can be resistance to expectations related to goals or activities that they themselves set, such as a child asking to go to the movies or shopping mall but then being unable to get in the car when the moment that they had chosen actually arrives. Also, children with PDA are often acutely aware of a low-key suggestion of a demand, and their reaction can be triggered very easily; avoidance can be very changeable, not only from one activity to another but from one moment in time to another. Isaac, a young person with PDA, said:

> I feel most anxious when I'm being pressed to do something that I feel I cannot do but the people around me don't understand because it seems such an easy thing... I know that I should be able to do it too but at the same time I just can't... It's difficult to explain, and to come to terms with myself.

Uses social strategies as a way of avoiding

Rather than using an outright "No," children with PDA tend to use socially strategic ways to avoid demands and expectations. That doesn't mean they won't on occasion give a direct "No" as a response. One of the notable characteristics of PDA is that there will often be an acknowledgment that they have been asked to do something, but they may present some reason why it is not possible for them to do so at this time. For instance, they may say that they can't walk to the classroom because their legs don't work, or they can't start a piece of work because they are much too busy doing something else, or they can't get ready for bed yet because the dog wouldn't like it. They may also use distraction such as "Are those new glasses you're wearing? They are a bit like mine. Let's swap and find out how well we can see using each other's." There can be extended procrastination, such as "I do remember saying that we could do that after this TV show but that was before I knew they would leave the episode on such a cliff hanger, so now I need to look online to find out if she dies." Or "We can do it in an hour/later/tomorrow/when Dad gets home..." Bearing in mind renegotiating like this may incorporate a number of versions, it can be exhausting for families and frustrating for siblings. In some instances, where a child has become particularly stressed, the avoidance can include more physically demonstrative behaviors.

Seemingly good social skills but lacks deeper social understanding

Children, teenagers and young adults with a PDA profile often come across as sociable, with more social awareness than some others with autism. This can, not surprisingly, contribute to confusion in some diagnosticians who may hold a narrower view of how autism profiles can present, so they miss or even misdiagnose those with PDA. However, on closer examination, in young people with PDA there will invariably be some core differences in their social understanding despite their surface sociability. They may indeed be socially motivated and to a degree socially skilled, but often there will be issues regarding predicting social outcomes (e.g. not understanding "If I do or say that thing how will it impact on the other person and how might they interpret my actions?") or navigating social relationships, especially if some social repair becomes necessary. For instance, someone with PDA may be successful at starting relationships but, if something goes wrong in the dynamic, could find it very hard to understand what's happened, why, and/or how they might repair the situation. Sometimes this leads to PDAers having serial best friends, where there can be an intense focus on one person, often to quite a controlling extent; then, if there's a disagreement, the friendship might end very abruptly. Managing conflict can also be difficult where someone with PDA might have genuine difficulty learning how to be assertive without being confrontational and thereby inadvertently damage their relationships.

Another aspect of this feature is that children with PDA may be good at tuning into different people. They may have learned that the best way to distract one teacher is to talk about baseball but the best way to distract another, who hates sports, is to talk about puppies. On the one hand this can enhance social relationships, on the other hand it provides social strategies to distract and divert from requests. Some PDA individuals camouflage their condition by appearing extremely compliant in certain situations, but this is invariably hard to sustain and causes emotional fallout later on. Typically, this describes children who "hold it all together" at school, containing their distress and masking their difficulties until they get home, where they feel sufficiently safe to express their feelings. Not surprisingly, it often leads to misunderstanding between educators and families, who describe quite a different child to the one the other party knows. It is vital that young people are seen holistically and that parents are listened to if their experience of their child differs from how they come across in other settings.

Children with PDA may have significant differences in their social identity. That is, they may not have a regard for social hierarchy or show any more respect to the school principal than to one of their friends or siblings. They may not find it easy to connect with their sense of self or to recognize the role they played in a social situation, especially where something has not gone well. This means they might have genuine difficulty taking responsibility for their own actions because they may view their actions in the context of the other person doing something they regard as irritating or unreasonable. They can then find themselves in situations of conflict where they may insist that someone only got hurt or an item only got damaged because the other person was being what they felt was provocative, without appreciating they could have responded differently themselves. As you might imagine, this can create some complicated interactions, particularly where other pupils or siblings are concerned. It may also create friction with some educators who feel compelled to appear "in charge" as the adult, and view children who challenge them as undermining instead of as individuals who need a different response.

Experiences mood swings

PDA individuals often experience sudden changes in mood or variability with their emotional regulation. Typically, this is as a reaction to a demand, whether that is an overt request, an implied expectation or even a demand they put on themselves. They may be hypervigilant, on the lookout for fresh demands coming their way. Not only can that be exhausting, but it can also mean they are highly sensitive to even the most subtle shift in a social situation. It means that sometimes a child is highly tuned into noticing "That's the look Mom usually has on her face just before she starts asking me to get ready for bed." Another aspect of mood swings can be that some individuals may experience particularly intensely felt emotions, yet at the same time they might find it really hard to recognize or to articulate their emotional states. All to say, this can frequently leave PDAers feeling emotionally overwhelmed.

Comfortable in role play and fantasy (more than many other autistic individuals)

This characteristic is notable in comparison to other children with autism spectrum conditions. Children with a PDA profile may not only enjoy pretend play but can sometimes get swept away into fantasy to the extent that they blur the lines between reality and pretend. Some young people with PDA can even create a persona for themselves and speak in a foreign accent or take on the role of an animal. Although being in a compliant role can offer a strategy that might encourage children to cooperate, we should take care that we continue to provide plenty of opportunities for them to check in with their authentic selves in order to protect their well-being and sense of self. On a positive note, viewed as a skill, it does open up avenues for other ways to engage children in learning and relationship building if they have an interest in drama, as well as offering potential future career pathways in creative arts.

Fascinations and fixations, often focused on people or social interests

With PDA, the way that "repetitive and restrictive" interests are often expressed is more likely to be centered around people or social activities.

Sometimes fascinations can be focused on a person known to the PDAer, and other times it might be a celebrity or someone only known from a distance. Sometimes the fascination can be really positive, other times it might be negative. There can be complications with both.

If, for example, a child has a positive fascination with another pupil at their school, that could present as them trying to emulate everything that other child does, has and wears, and risks them not only overwhelming the other child but also losing touch with who they really are themselves. It could also lead to them being more attached than the other child wants; they might be so protective of their friendship with that child that they prevent them playing with other children and try to guide or even control the choices their friend makes. What may be fueling this behavior is a delight in having a friend, a desire to enjoy their company and to protect their friendship. Unfortunately, the intensity of it can also cause unintended damage to a friendship.

If the fascination with another pupil is negative, it can lead to them being hypervigilant for irritants that child unintentionally causes. In some cases, it can even lead to situations where they provoke the other child, who may understandably feel targeted.

When a PDAer has a positive fixation on an adult it can create situations where those people are under a lot of pressure. If the fixation is on a preferred member of support staff they can feel that they should always be available. It can be hard if they are needed to work in a different class or to attend training, or if they are unwell. At home, often a child with PDA finds it very hard to separate from a parent, typically their mom, not only for extended periods of time or to attend school; in some families it's hard for them to be in a different room or to sleep separately even at older ages.

Fascinations with celebrities or historical figures are needless to say easier to manage because there is usually no direct interaction with those individuals. However, some of these fascinations can nonetheless raise other challenges, such as one young person whose special interest was in serial killers. A more positive example is another young person who was interested in the philanthropic work of a TV personality.

Experiences high anxiety, expressed as a drive to control or avoid

Having a PDA profile is intrinsically linked with experiencing high anxiety. Individuals with PDA talk about chronic physiological symptoms as well as emotional anxiety. These feelings are commonplace for many, who say things like Alice:

> I didn't know it was unusual to have a racing heart, sweaty palms and to feel sick most days until I talked about it. How was I meant to know not everyone felt like that? When I got to about 17 years old and I understood myself and my PDA better, I realized two things. One, that the feelings I had were called anxiety, and two, that as I got better at managing them, I didn't need to feel like that every day.

It is natural to try to control our environment when we become anxious or experience uncertainty, because we seek increased predictability in our situation to calm ourselves. The key difference in those with PDA is that this response is triggered much more quickly and much more frequently than in most other people. It should be noted when we are supporting children with PDA that their personal responses will be unique to them. They will have their own triggers, their own emotional and physiological reactions, and will cope with anxiety in their own way.

Being highly anxious can also have an impact on social environments, as it can be anxiety-provoking to spend time with people who are unregulated, impulsive and controlling. Obviously, that will have a significant impact on families as well as on other supporting adults. It is also likely to have a negative impact on the self-esteem of a PDAer themselves, who may find it hard to recognize or articulate how they feel but may be aware that their relationships are often tense and fragile.

WHAT CONSTITUTES DEMANDS AS EXPERIENCED BY PDA INDIVIDUALS?

There are many different forms of demands. As with all of us, young people with PDA are subject to expectations every day, and they will have their own reactions to them. Responses to expectations can depend on the context, fluctuating sensitivity or anxiety, who is asking and how they ask, whether the task is motivating or appealing, any associated social or emotional pressures, the state of their health, and their mood.

PDAers often describe the extent of their anxiety-driven avoidance and need for autonomy as overwhelming: "Demand avoidance makes it sound like I'm avoiding things on purpose, but I literally have no choice in it whatsoever" (Scott & Westcott 2019).

Another child described it thus: "It's like there's a train, and there is a driver at each end. Both drivers are pulling in a different direction so the train can't go anywhere. It just stays still. It freezes, like me" (PDA Society 2023).

Julia Daunt, an adult with PDA, says that her instinctive response to being asked to do something that is "not immediately appealing" is to say "No." She has wondered whether this is to protect her anxiety from rising, or to give herself more thinking time, or to see how she can twist or amend the request to regain an element of control to make it feel more acceptable.

It is useful to pause and reflect on the various types of demands that are made of children on an everyday basis. In a typical day before the child has even left the house, expectations can include:

- time to get up now
- use the toilet
- take your pajamas off
- get dressed
- come downstairs
- eat your breakfast
- have a drink
- brush your teeth
- get your coat
- get in the car.

And for many children with PDA, each one of these elements may incorporate layers of other demands; for example, "getting in the car" involves deciding which shoes and socks feel comfortable enough today, putting on two shoes and two socks, dealing with the transition of environment of walking out of the door, entering the car, putting on a seatbelt, anticipating the expectations of wherever they are going, and so on.

There are different types of demands we may experience, such as:

- **Direct demands:** These are the overt demands which are expressed directly. They include "Put that here please," "It's time to sit at the table for dinner," or "Write the date at the top of the page."
- **Implied demands:** These are expectations, which may not be said outright but are implicit in the body language or the situation. It may be the way the teacher starts tidying her desk and gathers up books ready to hand out to the class before introducing a piece of work, or it might be the implied demand to stand up to sing the national anthem.
- **Social demands:** These demands relate to social expectations, such as being expected to say hello or goodbye, not to

put your shoes on an armchair at a friend's house or to thank a relative for a birthday gift.

- **Legal demands:** These refer to keeping to speed limits on the road, not stealing, not damaging someone else's property, and so on.

- **Internal, physical demands:** Some people with PDA find it hard to get themselves food if their stomach is rumbling, to sleep when they are tired or to go to the toilet even when they feel an increasingly urgent need to do so. They may find these things easier to do before they get very hungry, thirsty or tired or need the toilet, because there is less of a demand associated with them.

- **Self-initiated demands:** This type of demand is often one of the most distressing to PDAers because it represents an obstacle to tasks, hobbies or activities that the individual would actually like to do. For instance, wanting to make a friend a birthday cake, which needs to be ready for the right day otherwise the moment is missed, can feel like a pressure that prevents the kind gesture from being possible.

- **Unexpected demands:** This refers to something happening that wasn't anticipated. Real life is full of these because plans sometimes change for all kinds of reasons. For PDAers that means they are not only having to cope with the uncertainty and the change it brings, but they also have to accommodate the loss of control: a double challenge.

Even taking account of the variation in an individual's emotional state and changing situations, it is not hard to see that there are going to be some times when the expectations on a young person quite simply exceed the capacity they have at that moment. Doubtless the same could be said of all of us, but the person with PDA is far more likely to reach that point sooner and more often than others.

OTHER DISTINGUISHING FEATURES

Although the following features do not form part of the key characteristics of PDA profiles, they are frequently observed. We may see potentially misleading first impressions. PDAers may manage social interactions well on first meetings, effectively using eye contact, expressing imaginative ideas, and using language-based humor such as puns. It is only with more in-depth observations that key differences in social understanding become apparent. There may also be issues regarding sensory processing differences. These can impact a variety of everyday tasks and activities, especially self-care and basic skills which, to some people, may seem out of sync with other areas of skill. They can also interfere with how PDA individuals manage transitions, organize tasks, interpret physical sensations and cope with sensory environments.

ADVERSE RESPONSE TO CONVENTIONAL TEACHING AND PARENTING APPROACHES

Many of the usual approaches used to teach children and to parent them are based on a format of the adult having most of the control and the child usually having to wait many years for a share of it. They are also based on rewards and consequences. Many neurotypical children respond positively to these approaches, when applied sensitively, modifying their behavior and making accommodations in the context of understanding the social environment around them. Furthermore, the strategies that are commonly helpful for other autistic individuals rely heavily upon clarity, order, structure and routine, which tend to need significant adaptation to be useful to those with PDA profiles.

We receive many requests for advice from educators who may have worked successfully for a number of years with other autistic pupils using these conventional strategies, who say they feel ill-equipped and confused when they realize they are struggling to connect with, least of all to teach, some children using their usual approaches.

The standard approaches tend to be not only less effective for children with PDA but can even cause greater distress and conflict. That's because they don't allow sufficient space for the choice, flexibility and autonomy that PDAers need. Too many strict boundaries can trigger high anxiety, which can lead children with PDA to resist and avoid with greater determination. Punishments are often ineffective because they rely on a child understanding the results of their own actions and being capable of moderating their behaviors or controlling their impulses to change how they react. These skills do not come easily to children with PDA, so expecting them not to act in accordance with something that is a core feature of their neurological profile is unlikely to be successful. Having said that, it is equally not in the best interests of children with PDA to remove all expectations and to have no boundaries. We need to aim at a sensitive and personalized blend of those elements using the principles of collaborative approaches to learning (Fidler & Christie 2019), which will be explored in detail in Chapter 4.

The ethos of the framework suggested in this book is not about imposing strategies on children in order to make them behave in a more neurotypical way. The focus is on recognizing the person for who they are and developing an awareness of the impact of their condition. The purpose is to help them understand themselves and promote better understanding of their profile in the people who support them. It is also so that, as they prepare for their adult lives ahead, we contribute to putting them in the best possible position, with access to opportunities for success across all areas of life.

CHAPTER 2

DIAGNOSING A PDA PROFILE

It is important for children to be understood as a whole person and to have their differences valued. If their autism or PDA profile is overlooked, they are not really seen; equally, if we only see their autism or PDA profile, they are not really seen either. Parents seek a diagnosis hoping it will provide an understanding of their child. Often that comes after trying many therapies, approaches and interventions, which leave them feeling they still have many unanswered questions and fuels their ongoing search.

Steph Curtis (2024) writes about the moment she came across PDA: "the 'standard' definitions of autism...did not describe our daughter very well...numerous late night research sessions on the internet led me to [PDA]. The descriptions of PDA seemed to fit our daughter like a glove in the way that the general autism indicators had not."

A diagnosis can validate what the parent and child have been experiencing. This is especially important for parents who might have felt dismissed or judged by professionals or by family members and is crucial in terms of signposting appropriate support. The psychologist Judy Eaton writes, "The longer parents of children with autism are denied access to considered and evidence-based support, the more likely families will become burnt out and suffer significant stress" (Eaton 2018).

For some, the impact of undiagnosed autism can contribute to depression, anxiety disorders or substance abuse, which may even lead to them requiring psychiatric treatment. These are not inevitable outcomes of an autism profile; they occur when individuals' needs have not been recognized or met. Debates about diagnosing PDA are further complicated due to evolving views of its place as an autism profile. Autism is a recognized diagnostic category, but interpreting more subtle or complex presentations of autism relies on the clinical expertise of diagnosticians, which is variable. Many families have been told that their child has features of autism but does not fit the criteria well enough to be formally diagnosed because they make eye contact or are too sociable or imaginative. An autism diagnosis can at least aid with accessing services, but often when children receive an autism diagnosis, the recommendations given may not suit the needs of an individual who fits the PDA profile. This is because they generally include recommendations for behavioral therapies, a highly structured environment, and an approach based on rewards and consequences, which do not work well for PDAers.

One parent reported:

> Initially I was relieved when we got a diagnosis of autism for my daughter because for years we had been told she was too sociable to be autistic. Now, the issue is that the strategies that have been recommended for autism don't work for her.

Hopefully, figuring out what is more effective is not something families need to do on their own, and they will find professionals able to partner with them as more learn about PDA.

Sometimes, by the time parents hear about PDA, the child may have received a combination of diagnoses, such as attention deficit hyperactivity disorder (ADHD), generalized anxiety disorder (GAD), oppositional defiant disorder (ODD), dysregulated mood disorder (DMD) and possibly autism (as ASD). Although some children do indeed have co-existing diagnoses, separating the presenting features of conditions can be less helpful than using one diagnostic formulation if doing so encompasses the whole child better.

Note too how prevalent the word "disorder" is in the above diagnoses, which often serves to compound negative and unhelpful connotations. It is important to reiterate that being neurodivergent "should not mean to convey that something is wrong within this person. Instead, it leads to an understanding that the person was born with a different type of nervous system, and it is incumbent on us to acknowledge that" (Henderson, Wayland & White 2023).

It is encouraging that there is a growing trend toward viewing autism from a perspective of difference rather than deficit. That is, to regard people with autism as having a different way of thinking, neither better nor worse than those without autism, but valuing what they bring to all of our lives. As Barry M. Prizant, speech-language pathologist and education consultant, says, "Autism isn't an illness. It is a different way of being human...to help we don't need to change them or fix [autistic people]. We need to work to understand them and then change what we do" (Prizant 2019).

THE DIAGNOSTIC PROCESS

It is helpful for parents to discuss procedures and approaches with the professional who is carrying out an assessment before they meet the child. Dr. Melissa Neff is a professional who had been at the forefront of diagnosing individuals with PDA in America before changing the direction of her career. In discussion with us, she has shared her insights about the process, suggesting that it would be helpful if parents are able to get answers to the following questions prior to the consultation:

- What is the clinician's general philosophy regarding the assessment process?
- What are the specifics of the assessment process?
- How is information from parents or others gathered and utilized?
- What are the professional's views regarding autism? Have they come across PDA? If so, what is their position on it?
- Does the professional use standard recommendations for autistic individuals? How individualized are these?
- What will happen if a child can't cooperate during the assessment or even attend in clinic?

Not every professional who offers evaluations and assessments is the right fit for a particular child or family. Parents may need to contact several professionals before selecting someone who is best suited to provide the service. Although it can be time-consuming, doing this groundwork will save time and money in the long run and can decrease the stress on the child. Plus, it can reduce unsuccessful consultations, which only leave a child more anxious and less trusting during future appointments.

In identifying effective evaluators, it is helpful to look for someone who will:

- listen to parents and view them as holding valuable knowledge about their child
- be open to considering PDA, even if they are less familiar with it
- be flexible—some days, testing may be brief or straightforward, and others it may need extra time because of anxiety
- be able to respond creatively and "go with the flow"
- be able and prepared to get into the child's world
- be able to present a sense of alliance in tasks presented and to share control of the session with the child
- negotiate—but not "trick" the child into cooperating

- be patient—to give additional processing time and use periods of quiet and pause to allow a suggestion to sit with a child until they are ready to move forward
- observe and pay attention to what the child does, as well as to what they do not do
- be compassionate—acknowledge the stress of attending assessments for the whole family.

Good assessment processes include the following:

- Interviews with parents, caregivers and family members. A complete developmental history should be included, paying attention to sensory issues.
- Objective tests (IQ, achievement, executive functioning, language and communication assessment).
- Diagnostic tools, such as the Autism Diagnostic Observation Schedule (ADOS; Lord, Rutter & Le Couter 1994; Lord et al. 2012); Monteiro Interview Guidelines for Diagnosing the Autism Spectrum (MIGDAS; Monteiro & Stegall 2018); the Childhood Autism Rating Scale (CARS; Schopler, Reichler & Rochen Renner 1988); the Diagnostic Interview for Social and Communication Disorders (DISCO; Wing et al. 2002); the Autism Diagnostic Interview—Revised (ADI-R; Rutter, Le Couter & Lord 2023); and the Developmental, Dimensional, and Diagnostic Interview (3Di; Santosh et al. 2009; Skuse et al. 2004). The ADOS tools differ from the others as they are not based on developmental data but look more closely at current behavior and skills. Any tool used forms the basis of a diagnosis but depends on the professional's interpretation and judgment of their findings. The ADOS is currently the most common tool for diagnosing autism in America.
- Parents and professionals may also refer to the Extreme Demand Avoidance Questionnaire (EDAQ), which is not a diagnostic tool, though it may be helpful. It was developed

as a research tool, but it can be used as part of an assessment to frame a discussion of PDA characteristics (O'Nions et al. 2021).

- Self-report and exploration of the person's internal experience. The evaluator should look at the individual's understanding of their emotions and any sensory differences experienced.
- Social and emotional tests that can inform about perspective-taking and empathy. The purpose is to look at how different diagnostic categories may overlap.
- Involvement of more than one professional to create a multidisciplinary view.
- Observations or input regarding the child in more than one setting, e.g. observation in a clinic as well as at home or school. Where direct observation is not feasible, there should be contributions from those who know the child in other contexts.

During an assessment, important information comes from the interaction between the child and the professional. The professional needs to pay very close attention to subtle clues and observe how they engage in general; how they listen and respond to additional information the evaluator is contributing; how they manage tasks both within and beyond their capability; how they transition between activities; different responses in child-led or adult-led activities; whether they appear hypervigilant to expectations or to sensory issues; and what strategies they may use to distract from or to avoid perceived demands. It is really important to try and recognize if a child is masking, though parental input may be needed to determine whether this is the case.

And finally, the diagnostic process should generate a jargon-free, written report which includes the following:

- reason for the referral, for example what has raised concern about the child's development and by whom

- procedures used or screening tools administered
- records and previous evaluations referred to
- individual/family background/relevant developmental and environmental history
- medical history, including medications, if relevant
- observations, for instance who carried out the observations, when and where
- summary of testing/findings
- summary/impressions of strengths and weaknesses; key themes that emerged during discussions
- diagnostic opinion and explanation of rationale
- discussion of other diagnoses to rule in or out; detail where there are overlapping diagnoses
- recommendations for interventions and supports at home or school, plus suggested therapies
- resources and links to useful services or publications.

The PDA Society in the UK have published guidelines for identifying and assessing PDA (PDA Society 2022). Among other useful advice it includes the diagram shown in Figure 2.1.

The PDA Society make clear that the diagram is intended as an illustrative aid that should be used in conjunction with other recognized systems plus clinical judgment—it is not a diagnostic tool.

Dr. Lisa Novak, an American licensed clinical psychologist, reflects these themes in discussion with the authors:

Diagnosing autism can be a tricky and nuanced task. The tools that were once considered the "gold standard" measures in our field do not always allow us to pick up on the more subtle differences of some individuals on the spectrum... Relying on a few standardized test scores can lead to missed diagnoses, as many individuals have spent their lives learning to "mask" or "camouflage" their neurodivergence to conform to the demands of a neurotypical world. As clinicians, it is our duty to remain curious about the how and the why of what our data tell us instead of relying on the numbers alone to inform our diagnoses.

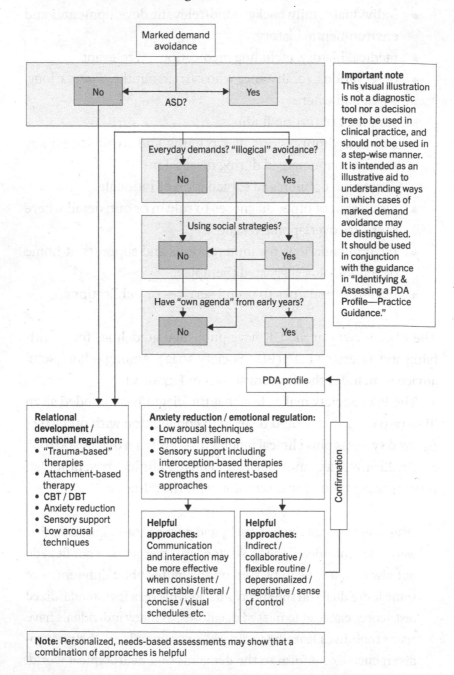

FIGURE 2.1 ILLUSTRATIVE GUIDE TO DISTINGUISHING PDA

Some practitioners in America have started to diagnose individuals with autism and then include the PDA profile within the detailed description. For instance, "X has autism, presenting with high anxiety and demand avoidance. The most helpful way to understand them is with reference to the PDA profile, and the best way to support them is by using recommended strategies associated with that profile." The recommendations that follow should then align with those set out in further chapters of this book.

DIAGNOSING GIRLS

Elizabeth Newson, in the first peer-reviewed published paper on PDA (Newson et al. 2003), noted that her initial figures regarding the gender ratio of PDA of 50:50 were significantly different from other presentations of autism. Autism prevalence data has come a long way in recent years, although there are still more males than females diagnosed. Some of the revised male-to-female figures suggest a ratio of 3:1 (Loomes, Hull & Mandy 2017).

With PDA profiles including seemingly better social skills, variability across settings such as a difference in behavior between school and home, mental health vulnerabilities, imaginative creativity, plus raised anxiety leading to avoidance and a need to control, there are often similarities drawn with other autistic girls. Gould and Ashton-Smith (2011) have suggested that PDA could be more typical of what has been referred to as a female autistic phenotype. It should be noted that the issue is often not so clearly defined and there will be individuals who did not fit this grouping.

Alongside this, the long-term effect of living with raised anxiety and concerted efforts to mask also needs to be recognized: "Girls with a PDA profile are likely to experience particularly high levels of anxiety which will, in turn, have an increased impact on their mental health" (Carpenter, Happe & Egerton 2019). It is not unusual, unfortunately, for autistic girls, including PDAers, to come to the attention of mental health services due to extreme behavioral responses or a mental health issue that is, in fact, an outcome of their underlying autism. There is also increasing concern for autistic girls regarding vulnerability to exploitation, eating disorders and self-harm.

It is vital that professionals, in their diagnostic processes and support interventions, understand autistic presentations in girls, particularly where they are subtly but significantly different from some of the more widely accepted male presentations of autism.

GETTING A DIAGNOSIS AS AN ADULT

Getting a diagnosis of PDA in a country where PDA is not widely recognized is complicated. Families often need to travel far from home to find a professional willing to diagnose PDA and to pay privately for the assessment. It can be an ordeal for the family and especially for the PDAer. Professionals rely on diagnostic criteria from the DSM-5-TR (American Psychiatric Association 2022) and ICD-11 (World Health Organization 2022), which currently do not include PDA.

Dr. Jessica Myszak, a psychologist in private practice in Illinois, described her experience undertaking diagnostic assessments for adults who fit the PDA profile. In discussion with us, she said:

> While many families of children with PDA learn about it and start using PDA parenting strategies long before they seek out a psychologist to evaluate their child for PDA, this is less often true with adults.
>
> Adults often seek an evaluation primarily for self-understanding, though a need for adaptations and accommodations at work or school can be important reasons as well... The relief at knowing

that they are not lazy, they are not stupid, and their brain just works differently is incredibly significant.

She adds, "Masking is an important component of assessment for autism and PDA in adults, and a psychological evaluation that does not address masking is incomplete."

Many PDA individuals are extremely articulate and can identify issues they encounter regarding everyday tasks such as managing hygiene, household chores and navigating social situations. Understanding the reason these activities may be complex for PDAers is key to supporting them effectively. One adult explained their feelings:

I felt such a relief when Dr. K told me about the PDA profile and that I am autistic. My whole life, I knew that I was different from most people and that things were harder and more confusing. Everyone just thought I was not trying hard enough. I felt so misunderstood.

Being able to view oneself in a neurodiversity affirmative way also protects individuals from gathering negative descriptions, whether those come from other people or the individual themselves: "Other benefits are less tangible but can be even more powerful... These include protection from inaccurate or pejorative labels...a sense of community with other people who share the neurotype, and greater understanding from their family, educators and healthcare professionals" (Henderson et al. 2023).

Many adults seek a formal diagnosis because they want confirmation of whether they are autistic and would like to be able to explain their differences to others with clarity and positivity. It is unfortunate that there are many barriers to easily accessing a diagnosis, especially for adults. In a perfect world, Americans would all have affordable access to a suitable professional who could offer adult diagnostic assessments.

Where some adults have been able to access a professional there are anecdotal examples of them finding that, like Colbie, "It was really beneficial to have a robust assessment by a professional. They asked questions I wouldn't have thought of on my own and they wanted to speak to other people who know me well, so they got different perspectives than just mine."

ACCESS ROUTES FOR AN ASSESSMENT

In America, individuals receive diagnoses in different ways, largely dependent on the type of health insurance and finances available. Larger cities have more options, but that does not necessarily mean that the options are better or more likely to be open to PDA. Anecdotal experiences are inevitably varied. Some families have disappointing experiences, like the parent who reported, "After three tries to get my daughter evaluated at a hospital with a well-respected autism clinic in my city, I was told that she is too uncooperative to be tested. They said there was nothing further they could offer us at this time."

Others have found the process more supportive and encouraging:

> Thanks so much for referring me to Dr. M. She did a complete reassessment of my daughter. It was clear that she listened and had read through the huge pile of documents that I sent her. She removed the prior diagnosis of ODD and diagnosed my daughter with autism and PDA. I feel so much better now that the assessment represents my child.

The following sections describe the potential routes to assessment in America.

Developmental pediatrician

Sometimes, a pediatrician will refer to a developmental pediatrician if they feel that particular expertise is needed due to the complexity of the child's presenting issues. Some developmental pediatricians will diagnose autism and may be open to considering PDA even if they don't include it in the official medical record. They will generally use diagnostic criteria from the DSM-5-TR or ICD-11. A pediatrician does not typically carry out the battery of testing typically used by a psychologist or interdisciplinary team.

Hospital clinic setting

These settings may have a multidisciplinary approach or autism team. They may have an autism-specific clinic and are often in big cities, so they can have long waiting lists. Because of the setting, they take private insurance and government-funded healthcare benefits. They usually have a rather prescriptive assessment process and use diagnostic criteria from the DSM-5. Large organizations often change their practice more slowly, so some may be more reluctant to consider PDA.

Independent private practice psychologists

These professionals may have more flexibility in scheduling and may take more time for each client. This could allow more time to explore and discuss PDA. Many private psychologists with good reputations have waiting lists, and they may or may not accept insurance, so this can be an expensive option, but many parents who can access this route have felt it was worth the expense.

Private practice clinic

Some of these are national "chains" with many different outpatient therapies, including speech and language therapy, occupational therapy, behavioral therapies, social skills groups and diagnostic assessments. These larger practices are more likely to take health insurance.

Psychiatrists

Many families consult with a psychiatrist initially because they are wondering if medication would be helpful for their child. Parents need to be able to develop a trusting and collaborative relationship with the psychiatrist in order to receive an accurate diagnosis, which can sometimes be made challenging by the short appointment times and a shortage of psychiatrists in many areas.

It is outside our specialism to express a view on medication use. Still, we would recommend a holistic, coordinated approach to prescribing, which incorporates regular medication reviews and feedback from the individual as part of the process.

Schools

The Individuals with Disabilities Education Act (IDEA) includes the "Child Find" mandate. Child Find requires all school districts to identify, locate and evaluate all children with disabilities, regardless of the complexity of their disabilities. This obligation to identify all children who may need special education services exists even if the school is not providing special education services to the child.

IDEA requires all states to develop and implement a practical method of determining which children with disabilities receive special education and related services and which children are not. This is laid out in Section 1412(a)(3); see Wright and Wright (2007), pp. 72, 206–207.

Schools may suggest that an existing student would benefit from an outside diagnostic assessment but are often careful about recommending having one done. Sometimes they will provide a list of professionals a family could contact.

Generally, schools will need to classify a student in order to offer them additional services. This is not a medical diagnosis. For a student to qualify for special education services, they need to meet the criteria for a specific condition. There are currently 14 categories, and autism is one of the recognized options (see box).

Individuals with Disabilities Act categories

IDEA categories include: (1) autism, (2) deaf-blindness, (3) deafness, (4) emotional disturbance, (5) hearing impairment, (6) intellectual disability, (7) multiple disabilities, (8) orthopedic impairment, (9) other health impairment (OHI), (10) specific learning disability (SLD), (11) speech or language impairment (SLI), (12) traumatic brain injury (TBI) and (13) visual impairment (including blindness).

There is the option to add (14) "developmental delay" as a disability category, at the discretion of the state. A child with developmental delay is one aged three through nine who experiences developmental delays in at least one of the following areas: physical development, cognitive development, communication development, social or emotional development, or adaptive development; and who, therefore, needs special education and related services.

Individuals with Disabilities Education Act (IDEA)

The move to gain wider recognition of PDA in America requires a broad view of autism. Previous preconceptions of autistic individuals who don't make eye contact, lack interest in social relationships, and are not imaginative or creative thinkers need to be challenged. This outdated picture of autism risks missing or misdiagnosing many people, especially girls and those with a PDA profile. That means they could potentially be excluded from getting the support they need, further harming their mental health. We also risk doing a disservice to autistic individuals and undervaluing their contribution to society overall.

CHAPTER 3

SUPPORTING FAMILIES AT HOME

Family life with a PDAer can be complex. It can feel confusing, unpredictable and frustrating. It can also be sweet, humorous and delightful. There are lots of wonderful moments but home life can also be very changeable.

Many parents of PDA children, teenagers and young adults describe their life at home as "walking on eggshells" or say they feel that their PDAer runs the household. It is probably the case that their child with a PDA profile has more control within the home than is usual in most families. However, a more helpful reflection is to work out *why* this has happened. It usually occurs in response to living with a very anxious child, who finds social relationships tough to navigate, and who is easily dysregulated and often exceptionally emotionally sensitive. This is a better way to explain why they're being controlling.

We are privileged enough to have been invited into the private lives of many families in two different countries. In our experience, the families who do best are those who practice self-care, carve out time for communicating and have a support system with friends and family as well as with understanding professionals. These factors are obviously ideal but are not always available, and rarely all at the same time. In addition, adopting a flexible parenting style that suits their child makes daily life easier, but most families have had to find out what works for them the hard way, by trial and error. What professionals need to appreciate is that parents, having lived with their child, are literally years ahead of them in this process, which means they carry a huge wealth of knowledge that will benefit everyone if it's shared. The goal of this chapter is to explore some of these approaches for parents, siblings, extended family members and the professionals who support them.

It is vital not only to support but also to inform parents and to learn about their individuals with them. One parent said, "As parents, we do better when we know better. Learning more about PDA has been transformational in helping us help our child."

Family life is rarely exactly how it was initially imagined when any parents first have children. Each child is an individual, and even when they are brought up in the same household with the same consistent parents, they will have their own unique experience. For families who have more than one child, there will be other people to take into account, and home life may be quite different from the one that the parents grew up in themselves. Tuning into our children, recognizing their own needs and personalities, can sometimes mean we need to re-cast our image of what family life looks like. Also, having more than one child, whether they have neurodivergent profiles or not, is no guarantee that the children will get along well. In addition, factors such as living circumstances, family culture, chronological place within the family structure, gender and educational experiences will all play a role in framing how a family works.

Other potentially challenging aspects of parenting a PDAer come from people outside the family. The impact of societal pressures and worries about what others think can bring additional stress. Well-meaning (but sometimes not so well-informed) acquaintances and relatives offer advice that may not even be asked for. However well-intentioned, without understanding PDA, much of it is unhelpful. The constant feeling of being judged can take an emotional toll on parents, leaving some feeling like they prefer to avoid going out or socializing.

Steph Curtis, mom to Sasha, reflected on her experience: "As I suspect is the case for most parents of children with additional needs, I often felt judged, and assumed that other people were thinking that I wasn't trying hard enough to manage behavior or teach my own child the basics" (Curtis 2024).

For some families, their everyday circle can become very small and intense. Families have reported that connecting with other parents of PDAers, even virtually, has been life changing. In her book *The Family Experience of PDA* (Fricker 2022), Eliza Fricker points out that "Parenting a child with PDA calls for empathy, kindness, calmness, compassion and humor, but it also requires connecting with other PDA parents because ultimately they 'get it.' They too are living it."

Another parent of a PDAer shared: "Until I heard about PDA and met other parents of children like my son, I thought I was the only person who lived this way. I feared neighbors would listen to my son yelling at me and judge me. Sharing my experiences with other parents has brought me great comfort. I no longer feel alone."

FAMILY LIFE

Parenting approaches that are required when raising a PDA child are highly individualized. PDAers need a specialized parenting style, as most tend not to respond to conventional approaches. This necessitates some emotional as well as practical adjustment. It requires ongoing flexibility and prioritization. Family members' needs can be conflicting, and parents are often stretched in their efforts to meet them all. One mother said:

> I never dreamed that I would be parenting this way. I had imagined myself being a strict disciplinarian like my parents were. Once I made the paradigm shift to parenting the way my daughter needs

me to, we began to share beautiful moments of closeness and many periods of shared laughter.

Having worked closely with many families over our careers, there are some repeating themes that parents talk about finding difficult. These include:

- creating a workable household routine with the changeable sensitivities of their PDAer
- prioritizing one person's needs over another's, which can leave parents feeling guilty or frustrated
- living in an unpredictable environment, which can be anxiety-provoking for everyone in the household
- managing attendance and engagement with education, whether that is school or via other education arrangements
- coping with additional workload regarding preparing separate meals and lengthy bedtime or bathtime routines along with chronic sleep deprivation
- dealing with pressures outside the immediate family, such as opinions of neighbors or extended family
- restructuring family finances if one parent is unable to work
- navigating a family schedule such as other children needing to be at school or activities on time
- attending appointments, haircuts, or going on trips
- managing meetings and paperwork regarding their child.

Educators and other professionals often ask parents personal questions about family life. They are subject to a higher degree of scrutiny into their home life than families usually experience. Having additional people "in your business" can feel intrusive, especially if you are not someone who is comfortable with others in your space and you value your privacy. Having a private life may not actually feel so private after all.

Even the homes where PDAers live can show the marks left by

meltdowns, with damage to doors that have been slammed once too often. Well-meaning, and hopefully supportive, professionals may end up visiting on days when a parent has focused on meeting the needs of their child so there are piles of laundry around or dirty dishes in the kitchen sink. There is no reason that should matter to the professional, but the parent may have preferred others not to see it.

Donald Winnicott, a British pediatrician and psychoanalyst, talked about children doing well if they have "good enough" parenting, meaning children growing up in environments where their basic needs were met: that is, that their caregivers are emotionally responsive and sensitive to their needs, and they are enabled to adapt and develop the skills they need as they mature (Winnicott 1971).

As parents, we tend to feel that being "good enough" is fine for other people, but we have higher expectations than that of ourselves. We can put untenable pressure on ourselves as parents in this respect, which is unnecessary and unfair. We can celebrate when we have managed to be better than "good enough," but we need not to be too harsh on ourselves when we have had a "good enough" day. We also need to allow ourselves odd slip-ups on the basis that we are only human, especially if we reflect and repair where needed.

Sometimes PDAers are emotionally closer to one parent than the other. They may find it hard to orient to two different styles of relating. They may focus on one person to help them feel safe and to co-regulate with them. This may cause the parent who is kept at a distance to feel hurt or left out. It's good to remember that the dynamic can shift over time, but in the meantime, it can be helpful if this parent adapts their role, maybe supporting the closer parent who might feel like they have no time for themselves, or maybe taking a bigger role in providing extra time to siblings. It can also be tough for the closer parent for different reasons, especially if the PDA child is quite controlling and ever-present. One mother said:

She tells me where to sit and is very controlling of what we watch on TV. If I try to go into another room she invariably follows me, even to the bathroom, and she can't cope if I try to go out of the house without her. She only wants me to put her to bed at night and sit with her until she falls asleep. Sometimes it makes me feel really bonded to her. Other times I feel stifled and almost like I have forgotten who I am if I'm not "just Mom."

In households with two adults, it is also essential to be careful not to overwhelm the PDA individual when they are dysregulated or on the path to losing regulation. Two adults talking to them can make them feel ganged-up on or overwhelmed. One adult at a time is usually a better strategy. Also, once a situation has ended with one parent, it is helpful to think about if or how the issue is revisited, when and by who. Sometimes it can be easier for the parent who wasn't involved to listen to the child's perspective, other times a PDAer may prefer resolution with the parent who was integral to the situation. Usually, they will need some time and distance from the event to be able to open up about it and it might help to talk it through in a low-key way, such as when on a car journey, in the bath, at bedtime, or while cooking together.

The more the environment can lower anxiety and make the PDA individual feel emotionally safe, the better they will be able to regulate their emotions. The focus needs to be on creating a supportive environment, not on expecting the PDAer to be different from the person they are.

Using declarative language and co-regulation can have a large impact in daily life. Declarative language is observational impersonal language that doesn't require a response and doesn't feature direct questions to which there may be perceived "right or wrong" answers. It can be an effective way to communicate with PDAers in a way that decreases demands (Murphy 2020).

Much can be done in the planning stage to increase the likelihood of success of outings, vacations and special occasions. It is understood that not all suggestions offered here will be possible or indeed suitable for all families. Readers should focus on the recommendations that are achievable and adapt them to their circumstances. Unfortunately, there will be some days when, despite every best effort to stay regulated and refer to recommended approaches, things just don't go well. Self-care and recuperation are essential at these times.

CHORES

Many parents worry that if their child does not do their share of household chores, they won't learn how to live independently. Siblings can also feel there is an imbalance of expectations, which can lead to friction and even resentment.

PDA individuals generally need to have things make sense to them to be able to perform unappealing tasks. For example, making one's bed in the morning when you are just going to get back into it that night may make little sense. The task has to be for a better reason than we are "supposed to" do it, or that an adult has requested it. One mother explained that when she showed her son his used cereal bowl after it had sat on the table for hours and all the leftover cereal pieces hardened like glue, he understood why it was important to rinse out the bowl after breakfast. The key is to present it as a teaching opportunity without judgment or pressure. Some children may enjoy getting involved in scientific experiments such as leaving one tooth in coke for a week and another in water to evidence the need for regular brushing and/or to avoid sugary drinks. Sometimes this might mean learning the hard way, as Peter's dad commented: "I'm sorry for him that he needed to get a fungal skin infection before he understood the need to wash more frequently, but at least he now views reminders about showering as helpful and kind rather than as needlessly demanding."

Children, teenagers and young adults with a PDA profile may

respond better to chores presented to them in a less personal, more indirect way. For instance, they may be resistant to putting shopping away or cleaning out the fridge at home but may be actively willing to do so for an elderly relative who they perceive needs the help more than Mom and Dad do. In these circumstances it is helpful to think about whether we are aiming at the PDAer learning the task (in which case it shouldn't matter whose house it happens in), or contributing to the workload in their own household (in which case that may need addressing in a different way, such as sharing who puts different types of groceries away, possibly even allowing the PDA individual to take a lead in delegating tasks).

Partnering and collaborating are effective strategies for getting chores done. Doing chores with the individual as an equal partner differs from them helping with the task. Giving control over timing or sequence, allowing processing time, letting the PDAer carry out the task in their own way (which may not always seem the most efficient) and giving choices can be helpful.

Examples are:

- folding laundry together while talking about an interest of theirs
- sharing a task, such as the child rinses the dishes, and the parent puts them in the dishwasher after offering the choice of tasks
- saying, "I am a bit worried that you will not be able to find all the pieces you need for your puzzle with so many other things on your bedroom floor. Should we pick up the things before dinner or after?"
- remarking, "It looks like the dog is getting anxious for dinner. How about you fill the bowl, and I will get him some water?"
- offering an indirect incentive, such as "Do you want to put the clothes in the washer or the drier, and I will do the other job? If I can get this chore done quickly, the sooner I will be free to play with you."

- proposing a game, such as "I wonder whether you can tidy the shoes in the hall away before I finish making the salad? Winner gets to choose what we buy for dessert."

Hygiene is often a challenging area for PDA individuals. It can be a perfect storm of sensory issues and demands. PDAers are most likely to perform hygiene tasks if connected to an event or activity of interest. Taking a shower because it is a general expectation is much less achievable than taking a shower in preparation for playing Dungeons and Dragons with a new group because you don't want to smell. Children may find it easier to bath with sensory toys in the water or may accept a form of washing with bubble bath in a kiddie pool.

ERRANDS AND OTHER OUTINGS

Running errands and having to go places may feel like unappealing chores for a PDA child. They may think that they are unnecessary or not a good use of anyone's time or energy. Busy environments may push the individual into social or sensory overload, so noting the importance of the task or outing at that time, alongside the PDA child's level of tolerance, is crucial. If the child has been picked up from school and is desperate to get to the safety of their bedroom, making stops on the way home might feel intolerable. Understandably, some tasks or outings have to be done on a schedule, especially when there are commitments for other siblings, but not all do. Often the better choice may be to plan ahead so that the PDA child doesn't have to accompany a family member and can stay home or do something else. This can save time arguing or negotiating. When they do have to go on an errand, understanding what could make the situation most comfortable is helpful. Equally, knowing what will make it worse is important. If stopping to get gas on the way to the grocery store is likely to make the situation worse, then filling the car can hopefully be planned for another time. Alternatively, if going to the gas station needs to be the priority errand, maybe a kind neighbor can pick up some groceries. These strategies are addressed in this way in the spirit of budgeting everyone's available time, energy and tolerance.

It might be useful to build in occasions to practice unplanned stops when the PDAers' tolerance can accommodate it, particularly where the stop presents an "upgrade." For example, "I know we had planned to go straight home but it's such a hot day. Should we have a surprise stop-off for ice cream?" That way there is a lesson about unplanned events being positive and stop-offs having a value.

To help errands make sense to a child with a PDA profile it may be helpful to highlight where the benefit lies. Benefits do not need to be directly personal for the young person; there are many ways for errands and chores to carry beneficial outcomes. For instance, doing something kind to please a loved one can make sense, just as much as coping with stopping at a shop for groceries so that there are favorite foods at home for dinner later. This is different from a reward for doing an errand.

Many PDAers like novelty, so long as the surprise is a pleasant one. You may be able to introduce a new outing that appeals, but it is probably wise to have done some basic research ahead of suggesting it, if only to be sure the activity is open that day and is affordable.

Considering some of the following can make this all easier:

- Bring drinks and snacks in case of hunger or thirst.
- Bring things to do if the person gets bored or needs distraction, such as a book, a small electronic device, and so on.
- Limit the number of errands or tasks to make it manageable.
- Plan in advance so extra tasks are not needed.
- Make sure that the errand is a priority and explain the reason for the errand.

- Balance the PDAer's level of tolerance with the importance of the demand.
- Build in making it worth their while if possible.
- Take a change of clothes, and/or alternative footwear.
- Give them a role on the journey, such as navigating or being the journey DJ. Maybe there could be a game where they host a pretend radio show, with phone-in interviews with the other passengers.
- Use the family car, if you have one, as a safe space. For instance, driving round the block with the temperature controlled and preferred music playing may be a good way to regulate.

Many parents describe how they need to consider so many details when they plan an outing, including what the weather may be like, what clothes their child may prefer, or whether they have the right brand of snack available. Not surprisingly, outings can be complex and exhausting, and because many variables are so delicate there is a lot that can go wrong. It's not that parents don't think about any of these things for their other children, it's the frequency, intensity and extent of potential reaction that is so different for a PDA child.

APPOINTMENTS

There are many different types of appointments that carry varying levels of priority and may be either much harder or much easier for some young people than others. Appointments may include important medical consultations as well as haircuts, or even times to meet a friend. As with other aspects of adapting approaches to meet the needs of a PDA person, it will always be best to understand the preferences and sensitivities of the individual before deciding what will be an effective way to support them.

In terms of formal appointments, some of the following may be helpful:

- Make professionals aware of the child's profile and what might help them. Maybe these points can be added to their notes. Try to open discussion about simple flexible accommodations such as entering a clinic by the back door, or even having the consultation in the parking lot. Don't forget, notes will need to be updated from time to time, and some professionals may need reminding to read what was previously agreed.

- Provide enough preparation to help the child anticipate what will happen and when they need to be ready, but not so much in advance that their anxiety becomes too high.

- Communicate in advance with the adults involved. For example, have written notes to give to medical professionals in case the child needs to leave early or there isn't time to talk through everything it would be helpful for them to know.

- Take another person/vehicle/activity along in case it's needed.

- Have low-arousal activities and environment before and after the appointment to keep the young person as regulated as possible. This can also regulate their supporting adults.

- Help the child understand the reason for the appointment—it's the purpose and benefit.

- Reduce waiting time or fill waiting time with calming preferred activities so that the child doesn't "feel" the empty space.

- Consider sensory needs. For example, the child could have their hair cut in comfortable clothes, then go straight home to have a shower or to a swimming pool so they can rinse off.

- Some dentists or hairstylists allow a child to have repeated appointments when they just sit in the chair or touch the tools before any treatment is even attempted. If they can explore the room and find something of interest to them, that can also help as a motivator or distraction.

- Have a plan B/emergency exit strategy for the child as well as for the adults.

HOLIDAYS AND SPECIAL OCCASIONS

Holidays and special events such as birthday celebrations and graduations are supposed to be fun, happy times. This adds pressure for everyone, and usually involves lots of people, a crowded space, noise, a car trip, fancier clothes, and different from usual food. There are often more substantial expectations to behave in a certain way. Some occasions may carry expectations to behave in a very unfamiliar way, especially if there is an element of ceremony involved. Although one PDA individual was delighted with being asked to be a bridesmaid at a family wedding, the wardrobe requirements were challenging for her. A settlement was agreed whereby she wore a long dress that covered her feet so she could wear her favorite slippers rather than heels. The pressure of these occasions for someone who fits the PDA profile may be even greater if they are the person being celebrated, because they will feel more of that pressure as the focus of attention.

A PDAer groom gave a charming speech at his wedding because, as he said, "My mom said I should say thank you," but he delivered his words in his own unique way. After praising his lovely bride, he went on to say that it was us, the guests, who should actually be thanking them because without him asking her to marry him we wouldn't even be having a party!

Exit strategies can be essential. Some families use a code word or gesture that any member can use to indicate "it's time to leave." There can also be a designated meeting place if someone needs to leave without feeling able to alert others. There just needs to be an agreed plan established before starting a stressful activity.

Simply having a plan can decrease the need for using one because it alleviates anxiety for everyone.

Sharing an individual's details with extended family members or family friends on these occasions is a personal choice and ideally should be made in collaboration with the PDAer. The benefit of sharing information is so that unnecessary stress is prevented or at least minimized. This could be reminding relatives not to request hugs at a family party, not to ask too many direct questions, not to expect greetings, not to ask how school is going or not to push the child to try the potato salad they made because it's a new recipe.

Frequently, a child who fits the PDA profile will agree to attend an outing or event but then feels unable to go when the time comes to set off to the event. This can be disappointing for parents and siblings and frustrating for the family, and often creates a logistical challenge if someone has to stay home with the PDA child and travel plans need to be rearranged. It's probably helpful if plans are made that are independent of other people's needs, for instance not agreeing to give someone else a ride or to be there at a specific time. It can even help to travel in two vehicles if that is an option, to accommodate different arrival and departure arrangements.

Parents may be tempted to pressure their children to change their minds, emphasize the benefits of going, or remind them that they had previously agreed to do so. Although very understandable, these responses generally don't help and can make the situation worse because they intensify the demand. The child most likely already feels badly about disappointing others and may be disappointed themselves that they are missing out. Reassuring them that they are understood and leaving options open for them to change their mind again and join the event later can be a more productive approach. It should be acknowledged that doing so does ask a lot of family members when they are experiencing their own emotions about the sudden change of plan as well. In this regard it may be wise to think of a reasonable Plan B that works well for the member of the family who stays home with their PDAer too.

VACATIONS

Going on a family vacation is similar to planning a special occasion, but is more multi-layered as there are often more "unknowns" and more logistics that are outside the control of any traveler. Also, they last longer than a few hours. The selection of the vacation spot is critical. If your PDA child melts in the heat and hates to be wet, a tropical beach vacation is obviously not the way to go. It can be hard to balance the needs of everyone, so sometimes creativity is needed. The key is flexible planning and ensuring that comfort and preferences can be met. Otherwise, it may not be the right time and may not be worth the money and stress at this time. Vacations are meant to be fun and relaxing, after all.

One mother of a PDA child noted:

> We finally had a good vacation. We rented a cabin in the woods about an hour from the city. For the first half, my husband and daughter went and had a great time. They did all kinds of nature activities. My son and I stayed home and listened to music and relaxed. We met halfway, then I went to the cabin with my daughter and my husband had quality time in the apartment with my son. They even went to some museums that we never have time for.

The PDA Society suggests key elements for planning special occasions, including preparation, accommodations, reducing uncertainty even around gifts, offering flexible choices, balancing family needs and managing anxiety.

SIBLINGS

Sibling relationships are very special and are unique to each family. Often siblings have strong bonds and are able to tune into each other. The sibling of a PDA child may see a situation from a different perspective than their parents and may be able to connect with their brother or sister to navigate all sorts of situations. They may also share the same sense of humor, which can help reduce stress and lift moods.

On the other hand, siblings of autistic children, including those with a PDA profile, may find they have to navigate issues related to the following:

- taking the role of helper, which can become their identity
- concerns about how their sibling's condition affects them now or in the future
- feeling pressure to be a "perfect child"
- guilt at surpassing the autistic sibling in some areas
- struggling with what they feel is "unfair treatment," such as the parents having different expectations for them and their sibling, and feeling their sibling "gets away with" things that they would be punished for
- feeling disappointment when they compare themselves to families of other friends
- having to bear the brunt of outbursts from their PDA sibling
- feeling tense when at home due to the unpredictable atmosphere
- feeling controlled by their sibling
- witnessing their sibling having a meltdown, which can be upsetting
- being upset by watching their parents struggling or stressed
- feeling left out and resentful because of the consistent and focused attention on their sibling
- feeling embarrassed when their friends come over to play if their sibling is displaying unusual, controlling or shocking behavior: some siblings miss out on playdates altogether
- feeling upset or frustrated by last-minute cancellations of family outings, or their sibling dictating activities.

In addition to this, PDA children can sometimes try to prevent or interrupt positive interactions between their siblings and parents, which can distress siblings. Some siblings may also have their own differences or challenges that go unrecognized. As a result of all the pressures on the sibling of a PDA child, some will harm themselves or use risky behavior.

As with their parents, siblings will feel better supported when their perspectives are recognized and listened to. It can be helpful to encourage siblings to express their feelings without guilt or blame. Maybe they can do so with a parent, but they may prefer to speak to someone outside the family unit. That might be a close family friend or relative, but it could also be a member of staff at school or a worker at a sibling support group or summer camp. In some cases, it might be a therapist, though it should not be interpreted that all siblings will need therapy. However, they may need support to recognize and understand their own emotions as well as to find helpful ways to express them. They may find personal outlets in sports or hobbies.

It will certainly be useful to talk to siblings about their own emotional wellbeing and what they can do to notice when they are becoming distressed as well as what helps to regulate them. These conversations are good to have with the rest of the family so there can be some agreement about strategies that work for everyone. For example, it might be that a sibling would really appreciate an outing once a month with their mom, just the two of them; it may be that the sibling wants to find a way to have an uninterrupted playdate at home, or that the sibling wants a private space in the house where they can go alone to play with LEGO® bricks or draw when they need some quiet time.

Although we want to encourage our children to be helpful and considerate, it can be easy to slide into having such high expectations of siblings that they either take on an unreasonable burden of responsibility or become resentful toward other family members.

Each family will need to work hard to get the balance to a comfortable place for them. Siblings can absolutely be celebrated for supporting their brother or sister, but they also need to be able sometimes to say they don't feel able to back down or to pick up the slack. When parents reward siblings it is important they do so both for helping with or accommodating the needs of their sibling *and* other actions, to avoid them feeling that they are only valued for helping with their sibling.

Finding ways to explain the characteristics of everyone in the family can create a positive model of understanding difference. It can also provide a framework for everyone to be able to express their needs and preferences and to have those woven into family life.

GRANDPARENTS AND OTHER EXTENDED FAMILY MEMBERS

Grandparents may need to work hard to balance their concern for their own child and that of their grandchild. It can be a double strain.

A grandmother once explained:

> When I am at my daughter's house, I tell her that everything will be fine and Ben will get much easier as he gets older. Then I come home and get in the shower, where I cry and cry. My heart breaks to see her so stressed and worried. I don't know how to help other than to be positive and encouraging.

Grandparents sometimes talk about being conscious that their adult child gets frustrated with their comments and that they feel like they say the wrong things. One reason this can happen may be that they have limited knowledge of the diagnosis, therapy and approaches that help. They may understandably be thinking back to their own experience of parenting or outdated attitudes about neurodiversity. One grandfather commented that if he were included in an Individualized Education Plan (IEP) meeting or therapy session, he felt his attempts to help could be more effective if he understood more about PDA—a very encouraging response which demonstrated his openness to learn.

Extended family members also benefit from more information about their relative who fits the PDA profile. If they don't understand them and only see them rarely, such as once a year on holidays, they may be uncomfortable and might not know how best to interact positively. Cousins can be a valuable resource for children and adolescents who struggle with friendship and social skills. Aunts and uncles can sometimes bring up topics for discussion in the context of a loving nurturing extended family that a child may be resistant to talking to their parents about.

Having a PDA person in the family impacts all those involved. The more understanding that exists, the better. Families who can talk openly about their thoughts and feelings have a significant advantage on the road to a happier family life.

WHAT CAN PROFESSIONALS DO TO SUPPORT FAMILIES?

Aside from the not inconsiderable task of taking care of their autistic children as well as the other aspects of everyday life as an adult, parents of children with additional needs can quickly become overwhelmed with paperwork, meetings, appointments and legal cases related to their child, which can soon feel like a full-time job. This can dominate parents' lives, especially if the workload falls mostly on one parent. Alice Running, a parent of two boys with PDA profiles, says, "In supporting my children through several episodes of crisis, I have lost friends, relationships, jobs and my home. I have spent my savings on obtaining assessments, reports and legal advice. I have been exhausted for a long time" (Running 2022).

This is a fraught and unsustainable position for families to find themselves in, and professionals have a responsibility to understand and to support the whole family, not only the child, when they become involved. Failing to do so can inadvertently contribute to untenable pressure on the family and ultimately on the child themselves, so services need to look carefully and creatively at providing support. This can be as simple as providing time to just listen to parents. It is also important to listen to what they are describing without judgment, but with an openness to understanding their perspective. Collaborative work is only possible when people can be honest with each other and feel heard. Often families have had previously difficult experiences with professional services and may have been under a lot of pressure before new services become involved, so creating an atmosphere of mutual trust and respect is a crucial starting place.

Putting parents in touch with other families can be beneficial too, and professionals may be in a good position to facilitate parent support groups that provide training and opportunities to share helpful resources. For many families, simply meeting others who have similar experiences of parenting children with a PDA profile can be extremely validating and encouraging.

There is an often used metaphor about in-flight emergency advice for parents to apply their own oxygen mask first before they try to help their children. The principle of this is that adults will pass out quickly without oxygen, at which point they will not be able to help their children or themselves. We recognize that PDAers are prone to high anxiety and frequent dysregulation, so it makes sense that the better supported the people who live with them are, the more settled they are themselves, which means they are in a better position to help their children regulate. That way everyone can not only survive but thrive.

POSITIVE ASPECTS OF A PDA
INDIVIDUAL IN THE FAMILY

It is easy to find ourselves looking at the difficulties that impact families, but we also want to be focusing on PDA as a model of difference. It is true that some differences bring their issues, but there is also plenty to celebrate.

PDA individuals who are regulated and comfortable can be extremely good company. They can have an excellent sense of humor and very entertaining ways to engage. PDAers are often not afraid of challenging accepted norms, so they can be great at thinking outside the box. For example, they may find the standard rules of a board game too restricting and demanding but may be able to devise their own, with fun forfeits that really bring the family together and set some new family traditions. Similarly, they are not usually put off by the social hierarchy that can stifle the voices of other children, so they may be bold enough to suggest new and different ways of doing things, whether that's new arrangements on Thanksgiving or adventure activities the family can try. Not everyone finds creative thinking easy, so we should celebrate those among us who can encourage us all to do more of it.

CHAPTER 4

APPROACHES TO FACILITATE LEARNING

The approaches outlined within this chapter are aimed at facilitating learning. It must be noted that learning happens in a wide variety of situations, whether that is formal education settings, social situations or at home. Every experience is a learning opportunity, including those that go well and those that don't. All experiences have the potential to teach us something, but it's most likely that we learn when the supporting approaches suit our learning style. Making adaptations to align with individuals' learning needs is the basis of this chapter. There is not a clear dividing line between the strategies that work well for a PDAer or for other anxious autistic learners, but there are key principles that inform our approaches. The important work here focuses on *connecting* with the learner and thinking about *how* we do what we do as well as *why* we do it.

PDA is dimensional, and the same is true of approaches that support PDAers. We will need to use a combination of approaches that take into account the individual's unique profile, and it is likely that we will need to personalize many of these and be prepared to disregard others. The more "tried and tested" autism-friendly strategies tend to be very direct in nature. They are usually characterized by being really clear, often in concise, visual form; they tell a young person what is going to happen, when and how. They are very effective in providing predictability and clear expectations, but this is the very reason they are less suitable for PDA individuals. Too often they are perceived as a list of demands with little or no room for choice or negotiation. We are not saying these strategies are of no use for autistic individuals, just that they are less so for those with a PDA profile. What matters is to know why you are using certain strategies, with whom, and what rationale or evidence there is that they are a good match for that person's profile.

Regular school attendance works for some but is not right for everyone. There is some very unfortunate language used regarding the educational experiences of children, teenagers and young adults with PDA profiles. Terms such as "school refusal" are unhelpful for children, families and professionals. "School refusal" implies that the child could be persuaded to go to school and to attend regularly if only they were more strongly encouraged or even forced to do so by families who are "not trying hard enough." Or that the PDA child is just being willful and defiant. Both not true. Needs-related non-attendance would be a more useful way of framing the reason that a PDA child is currently unable to attend school. It is certainly not their fault that their needs are not being sufficiently understood or met. If a child is resistant to going to school, it is curious how some people will be quick to judge parents or even the individual themselves, rather than to look at the wider picture of what their experience of school feels like to them. Furthermore, being in a setting that doesn't work for a young person can have a detrimental impact on their mental health as well as on the wellbeing of their family. It can leave some PDAers feeling that they are the problem, or that they have failed, when it is the system that has failed them.

Fortunately, there are some more positive educators who are open to adapting their practice, such as the teacher who reported:

We had been told that Wyatt was autistic, but his needs were very different to our other autistic students and it was confusing that our usual autism strategies were not helping. In fact, they seemed to be making things worse. Searching for answers led us to PDA.

Seeing him through this lens enabled us to understand him better and successfully adapt our practices by building trust and embracing a flexible and collaborative approach.

We have discussed reflecting on what is behind the responses of the child or young person (in the case of PDA it is invariably anxiety, hypersensitivity and/or overload), but it is also important to reflect on what may be driving the responses of the supporting adults, especially those working in school settings. Education professionals may feel considerable pressure to produce performance evidence in their students, they may feel scrutinized regarding how they implement school behavior policies, and they may have been advised to tighten up on the conventional autism strategies, even when these seem not to be effective, and only lead to increased levels of demand and inflexibility. Of course, these factors of practice can be explored and challenged, but the educator may need support and guidance from their colleagues and managers to be able to do so positively. Adults who are supporting PDAers at home may feel pressures from other members of the family, who might struggle to make sense of why their child is reacting the way they do, or disagree with parenting or homeschooling choices.

WHAT IS THE IMPACT OF PDA ON LEARNING?

Teaching and learning are separate, though related, processes. Learning happens when we synthesize new information, understand a concept, revise a developing skill or reach levels of expertise by ongoing practice. Teaching happens when someone facilitates learning, but equally, an experience or an event can also "teach us something." *Pedagogy* is the term used to describe the art of teaching and there are many approaches and contexts for teaching. The relationship between teaching and learning is delicate and personal, as is the relationship between teacher and learner.

Given that PDA is part of the autism spectrum, it is not surprising that busy classroom environments can impact learners with a PDA profile in many of the same ways as other autistic students. They may find navigating social relationships difficult, they may have trouble predicting outcomes, they may be prone to sensory sensitivities, and the anxiety they experience can lead to demand-avoidant or controlling behavior in an attempt to mitigate that anxiety. In addition, they may find working in a group challenging and school tests might be very anxiety-provoking. They may feel driven to produce "perfect" work, and anything less than the unrealistically high standard they set themselves is felt to represent a personal failure. When this happens, it is not unusual for students to destroy their work or to sabotage their own projects.

Although Eli, now 24, has a full-time job and has found ways to manage his perfectionist tendencies, he says:

> I like to do a good job and to stick with something until it's finished. My boss knows I have high standards so he trusts me to get on with my tasks. Sometimes I find it hard to go home when I'm meant to at the end of a shift because I haven't got everything perfect. I'm torn between feeling bad if the job's not right, and feeling exhausted because I'm always working extra time.

For a student with a PDA profile their fluctuating sensitivity to having something expected of them is often more acute than is proportionate to the content of a particular demand. That is why it doesn't always matter if the details of the task are aversive or not; it's the pressure of the perceived demand that is being responded to. They may be able to carry out a task one day but not another, or they might complete a complex task based on a personal interest yet get stuck halfway through getting dressed. They may benefit from increased adult support, yet feel too socially exposed to be singled out for 1:1 interventions.

On top of this, there are multiple social and sensory reasons why

PDAers might find the average classroom learning environment overwhelming. All of these factors do not mean they are not capable of learning, just that they need enough reasonable adjustments in order to access learning.

WHAT IS A DEMAND?

Demands can be multi-faceted and will be perceived differently by different individuals. We have already looked at some of the types of demand in Chapter 1. First, we should acknowledge that the closer to overload a person is, the faster they will react to yet another expectation. They will also react more extremely if they have little emotional capacity remaining. Second, we all regard everyday demands differently. If the same problem is presented to two people, one may take it on as an ordinary task that's barely noticed, and another may be immediately overwhelmed and feel unable to function. This doesn't only relate to the content of the task but also to the timing and the style in which it was presented, and may reflect the relationship with whoever is asking. In addition to this, there are further expectations we place on ourselves. Usually this sort of demand starts with "I should be doing..." or "I know I said I would do..." For some people, the self-imposed pressures of these demands and the negative feelings occurring if tasks have not been completed satisfactorily contribute to overload.

PDA individuals may also be sensitive to the social and sensory demands of their environment. All these factors contribute to the background context for any everyday request. Individual personality, social dynamics and age-related expectations have a role too.

If we consider an ordinary school day, the demands and expectations begin upon waking:

- time to wake up
- get out of bed

- interact with family
- get washed, use the toilet and brush your teeth
- have something to eat and drink
- make your bed
- get dressed
- get your schoolbag and lunch
- go to the school bus
- interact with the driver and other students
- get off the bus and into school
- hang up your coat, find your class, take your seat.

What you will doubtless have noticed is that many of the points above have more than one element to them. Indeed, some of the seemingly straightforward ones have a lot of smaller parts to them. These represent demands within demands; for instance, getting dressed requires putting on various items of clothes. The examples given here are just some of the demands made of a student before they even arrive in front of their teacher. It is paramount for school staff to appreciate that the start of the school day is not the start of the day's demands. Even for those children who are homeschooled, there continue to be everyday elements of an ordinary day that carry some degree of expectation.

ATTITUDES AND VALUES

This section highlights key elements of effective support for students with a PDA profile whatever their education settings. It goes without saying that they will need to be individualized and tailored to the pupil; it is the core principles that are set out here. Underpinning the approaches are a set of values that should be evident in organizations and in staff teams, and in good practice across all services involved.

Teams of supporting adults will be most effective if they have a commitment to:

- viewing autism and PDA profiles from the perspective of difference, not of deficit
- building positive relationships with families
- building rapport with students
- being prepared to be creative and flexible in response to the individual's needs, and being open to ask themselves if there are alternative ways to reach a mutually satisfactory conclusion to a given task
- considering whether the student's usual schedule is working for them or needs altering
- being conscious of what's contributing to responses, and being ready to ask themselves, "Why are they doing/not doing this? Why now? What does that teach me about them? What does the child's response teach us about how they need us to adjust?"
- adults being reflective regarding their own responses, and asking themselves, "Why am I reacting like this? Is there an alternative approach I could try? What is my response bringing to this interaction? Is there some key background information that I don't have right now which would help inform my response?"
- checking in with wellbeing: remaining aware of the variable emotional capacity of students at any time, seeking advice from others who know them better if unsure, and endeavoring not to overload them with more than they can manage just now
- keeping in mind the student's holistic profile: being conscious of their personality and the impact of their PDA as well as other aspects of their circumstances, such as unexpected changes, health issues or current worries.

CHOOSING PRIORITIES

It may sound obvious to suggest that educators should be identifying learning priorities for their students, but there are a couple of additional features to bear in mind when we are supporting PDAers. Most important is our start point, which should include understanding what has characterized their previous life experiences, and specifically their previous school experiences. We should also understand the wider context of the person, which means liaising with their family to develop a shared set of priorities. Within the learning aims, we should consider a curriculum that is broader than academic subjects and we should take account of personal development goals. Furthermore, we need to look not only at what are high priorities, but also at those we have collaboratively agreed are low priorities at this point in time. Determining something as a low priority does not mean it has to remain so long-term, but that for now we can let it go. For instance, as a child settles into a new education setting, we may feel it is a low priority that they arrive precisely on time and bring all their own books, technology or writing utensils. Medium priorities may be identified as those that a child is starting to manage and would benefit from extending. If they are being homeschooled, a high priority may be that they engage with some kind of educational experience each day, however briefly that may be. If they are at home because of burnout, a high priority may be that they meet their basic needs of eating or of self-care, and maybe that they interact with at least one other individual each day.

Within the PDA literature there are examples of priority rating charts. These are simple tools designed to provide a framework for collaborative discussions. Completing a priority rating chart (see below for an example) is best done with all those involved. It should include the voice of the student and should have a review time scale set.

After completing a priority rating chart, a teacher said:

This is such a simple tool but it has been so effective! It's helped us really discuss what matters, what doesn't matter for now, and to understand the difference between the two. It has taken pressure off Alex as well as off me as their teacher, so that all our energies are going where they need them most.

A parent reflecting on doing a chart for homeschooling commented:

It has helped us understand more about why our daughter found attending school so tough, when we realized how many unnecessary "priorities" were being expected there. Now we have chosen home education, we can shift the focus onto more targeted and personal issues that prioritize her wellbeing and engagement.

When exploring priorities, it may be helpful to refer to the work of Ross Greene, a clinical psychologist, whose main principle is that "children do well if they can." He explains, "if your child could do well, he would do well. If he could handle disagreements and adults setting limits and demands being placed on him without exploding, he'd do it" (Greene 2005).

When a child is not doing well, he suggests, there may be key skills that are lagging and are getting in the way of them doing well. Considering what skills, to use Ross Greene's word, may be "lagging" can inform our discussions about identifying priorities. Rather than selecting as a priority that a child refrains from doing the thing they don't have the skills to refrain from, the focus is instead on teaching them the skills they need. If we change the lens through which we view a child, we can determine how to support them better to gain these skills, rather than punish them for not having yet acquired them.

PRIORITY RATING CHART

Student name . . . .

Education group, age . . . .

How important is it that the student...?	Priority level	Comments, rationale and plan
Completed in consultation with:	Date:	Next review of the above planned for:
. . . .	. . . .	. . . .

IMPLEMENTING PRIORITIES

Once priorities have been identified the next step is about implementation. Who is going to deliver what has been decided, where, when, with what support? And how will we know if this has been effective or if the young person has made any progress? Whatever the setting, including homeschooling, these are important questions to address so that we know we are meeting an individual's needs and positively contributing to their learning. That is not to say that learning needs to emphasize academic subjects or qualifications, although these opportunities should not be limited, but that what is taught should reflect every realm of learning which will be satisfying and positive, and can support the young person to thrive as they mature.

What is taught will be determined by what emerges from the profiling tool that you will find in Chapter 7, and the prioritization tools in this chapter. Not everything that is a medium or low priority will be excluded from learning opportunities, but they will not have the same level of attention as the high priorities. These may comprise areas of learning that continue to be important to offer to a child, but without the focus that accompanies more targeted ones. For example, at home, even if you have decided that it is a medium priority that the child clears up their dirty dishes, you may still open the dishwasher and comment that there's space for their dishes, but said without any expectation they follow through. In a classroom, you may present a piece of work with a range of optional responses, one of which is to postpone it, possibly even indefinitely. These broad principles should apply to teaching across all settings and age groups, whether the learning is happening at home, in the community or within an education setting.

Who teaches and where that happens will also need careful consideration. Relationships are crucial to engagement and therefore to making progress for learners with a PDA profile. Any and every experience is a potential learning experience; the skill for supporting adults is in being able to recognize these opportunities and make the most of them where they naturally occur. Sometimes this means adults need to deviate from the direction they had planned. Amending plans in the moment is not always easy, but when we get better at doing it smoothly, we can find that each day offers many chances to learn or to reinforce a skill, just in a different order, or venue, or via a different activity than the one we had anticipated.

For example, in a home or community setting, you may have planned to visit an aquarium to reflect an interest in fish, only to find out that due to unforeseen circumstances the center is shut that afternoon. The learning opportunities arising from this could include: contacting the enquiry email address or telephoning to find out when the center will be open again; finding an alternative place to visit and planning the journey and costs involved; expressing emotion and exploring regulation techniques which can be practiced in a real-time situation. In a school classroom it may represent small adaptations such as taking the learning task outside onto the yard, or using the school pet as a focus for the activity. It might also mean adjusting the daily schedule so that the order of lessons that day is swapped. For education professionals, teaching in this flexible way requires adaptation on the part of the staff and often also needs support from understanding administrators who recognize the different needs of pupils with a PDA profile. Staff training can be helpful in this regard. Adults who are well tuned into the child's fluctuating sensitivities tend to be good at reading when they can stretch learning, whatever the task at hand.

How information is presented is key to engagement with PDAers. Creating a sense of alliance with the young person whereby tasks are approached from the perspective of "How are *we* going to do this together?" rather than "I'm the adult here to deliver teaching resources and it's up to you to learn" is going to be much more effective. Again, even though you will need to develop the detail to suit the person, there are some core principles. In general, approaches that are based on personal interests; are well timed to coincide with the person being sufficiently well regulated to engage; are indirect; allow additional processing time; that include humor, drama and challenges that appeal; that avoid unnecessary confrontation or overload; and that promote emotional wellbeing are going to be preferable.

ORGANIZATIONAL ACCOMMODATIONS

Typical school environments present children with a constant stream of expectations, from what time they arrive, where they sit, what they eat and what is on their timetable. Whereas this can work for enough of the pupils enough of the time, there are a number of students who find this very challenging, including those with a PDA profile. One of the reasons it can be tough is that most school systems are not individualized or flexible enough. Schools can make a positive and effective difference if they make reasonable adjustments, such as:

- allowing the student to enter/exit through a quieter door, possibly a few minutes before or after the larger crowds have arrived or left
- implementing flexible elements to schedules, for example if the person needs recovery space or needs access to regulating activities to prepare for the next lesson, or if they will benefit from additional time to study a special interest
- providing wellbeing sessions during the school day
- having a key trusted member of staff to check in with as often as necessary

- having an agreed exit strategy in case they are reaching overload
- having flexible arrangements regarding completing homework or school assignments.

The more that children and young people are involved in devising accommodations to their day, the more they will improve their understanding of why and when they are needed and be able to start taking charge of implementing them independently as they mature.

The example of a high school student may be helpful in prompting and formalizing accommodations.

Accommodation plans should reflect collaborative discussion about what will best support the student, where possible should include the student's views or preferences, and should be regularly reviewed.

ACCOMMODATION PLAN

Situation and sensitivity	Accommodation	Agreed with who and when?	Date reviewed and whether still required
Arrival at school at the same time as others—social environment too busy.	Arrives 15 minutes after others, and stays an extra 15 minutes at the end of the day. Staying later allows for the corridors to empty and provides tutor time to chat about the day.	Mr. Rodriguez 9/20/24	
Working in a group. May be difficult if paired with students from Group B.	To be paired with Group A students only. Mrs. Sanchez to facilitate task delegation in group or paired work tasks. Most delegated tasks to be carried out separately, then brought back to the group.	Mr. Collins Mrs. Sanchez 9/12/24	
Completing pieces of homework. There are obstacles (emotional and organizational) to doing homework at home.	Expectations to complete homework at home currently suspended. Any work done outside class to be accepted without punishment, regardless of quality. History lessons currently dropped from schedule so "homework" in other subjects can be done in resource room during these slots. Support available at those times from Mrs. Sanchez.	Mr. Lucas Mrs. Sanchez 9/12/24	
Getting changed for PE. Often problematic due to busy social environment and sensory sensitivities in changing room.	Arrives wearing suitable clothes and footwear appropriate to gym activities on days when required. Spare clothes to be kept in locker in case needed (mom to facilitate this). Access to library before sports and after if required.	Mrs. Sanchez Mrs. Kim (mom) Coach Williams 9/23/24	

BUILDING POSITIVE RELATIONSHIPS

We cannot emphasize enough the importance of building positive relationships with PDAers. Like all of us, children, teenagers and young adults with a PDA profile do best when they are in nurturing relationships where they feel understood and accepted for who they are. Supporting adults need to give out signals that leave the PDA person feeling "Hey, this person enjoys being with me, they want to know me better, they are interested in me."

Zack, a teenage PDAer, following a lengthy and sometimes challenging period of time settling into a new educational setting, said, "I know I sometimes give you all a hard time, but this is the first school I've ever been to where the teachers actually like me. I've never felt like teachers want to spend time with me before." Although that is a sad reflection on his previous placement, it was a pivotal time in turning his school experience around.

Facilitating positive relationships between a PDA child and other children is also important. It should be remembered that some PDAers prefer the company of children who are either younger or older than them, depending on their own sensitivities. This suggests that supporting adults need to think creatively about class cohorts and social grouping.

SELECTING SUPPORTING ADULTS CAREFULLY

We all have different personalities, interests and strengths. Ideally a staff team will include a range of individuals and will be able to incorporate the best personality matches for their PDAers. Typically, adults who are creative, who are conscious of pupil wellbeing, who are prepared to be flexible and playful, who are comfortable with facilitating more control for students than may be usual, and who may have overlapping interests or areas of expertise with them will be well suited.

When a child is being homeschooled there will be a smaller pool of supporting adults who are available to work with them. In school settings there will be a variety of adults who creative administrators could make available.

In schools it can help if a student starts with a very small team of staff around them who understand them and connect with them well. Over time, it is important that this team is extended, not only to give the child a wider social experience but also to have a larger bank of adults who can work effectively and cover each other as required. Working very closely with a PDA child can be quite an intense experience, so spreading the load can also help staff energy levels. Swapping adults and introducing a different but equally safe person can also be a positive way to move on from a situation that has become "stuck." As children mature, it will also help them access a wider range of activities and experiences if they are not overly dependent on a very small number of supporting adults. It can be complicated to extend the number of safe people that a homeschooled child can interact with, especially if the family do not have a wider network or where there are no siblings. In these cases, it can be beneficial to think creatively and consider opportunities in the community, such as swimming or youth groups.

TUNING IN

Clearly, PDAers are first and foremost individuals; often particularly individual individuals. We have highlighted the importance of building trusting relationships with them. Parents will know their children in a way that professionals will never be able to, and will usually be finely tuned into the small changes and nuances of behavioral responses. Professionals will be able to offer a broad knowledge, gained from working with a number of children and families. Professionals can of course get to know children well, and may be familiar with how a child reacts in situations outside the family home, such as at school. We need to share our expertise. Doing so means that we need to raise our awareness of the subtle signals that indicate how someone is feeling. Some children may lower their head, close their eyes and set their jaw when they are in pain; others may start to rub their fingertips with their thumbs when they need the bathroom, or tap their feet and jiggle their legs when they're excited. There are no rulebooks for reading these signals, but there may be general patterns. Often supporting adults rely heavily on "instinct." If we can refine our instinctive processing and articulate what we are noticing, then we can share our under-standing with other people, especially when children are less able to express themselves verbally in moments of heightened emotion.

It is also helpful to take care that we have the relevant back-ground information needed to support the person we are with. That may mean checking in with whoever was last with them who may be able to inform us whether they might be hungry, distracted by a sensory sensitivity, halfway through a game, or waiting to hear back about something. It will be useful to confirm any changes they have had to accommodate that day, such as: Was the school bus late? Is there a substitute teacher in class? Is soccer practice cancelled? This context is extremely useful in helping us navigate our session together.

As we get to know PDAers better we should also bear in mind that they may be masking, in which case we should not make assumptions about how they really feel on the basis of how they seem to be.

A core element of approaches to support PDA individuals that runs throughout much of the literature is the notion of tuning into how the young person is feeling and adapting our response accordingly by thinking of two dials (see Figure 4.1). These are metaphorical dials, which simultaneously measure an individual's tolerance to demands (including external, self-imposed and per-ceived demands), and the amount of demand that is being pre-sented to them (including overt requests, indirect expectations and environmental factors). The aim is to synchronize the dials so that the amount of demand being presented does not exceed the capacity to tolerate it at any given time. Not surprisingly, this is easier said than done in some situations, but retaining the aspiration to do so is an important guiding principle of interacting with PDAers.

There may be times when our dials are not well synchronized because we have misjudged something, or failed to read the subtle signals. There may be times when the young person's state of regulation has altered very quickly with very few observable indicators. There may be times when, despite our best efforts, we have not been able to reduce demands sufficiently to align with their emotional state, maybe because there are some circumstantial factors outside our control, or there is a non-negotiable safety issue. It is important not to give up should these situations occur. We can still aim to repair the interaction and to do what we can to recalibrate our dials as soon as feasible, to regain that equilibrium.

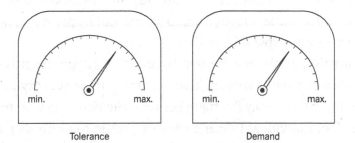

FIGURE 4.1 SYNCHRONIZING THE ADULT'S EXPECTATIONS WITH
THE CHILD'S TOLERANCE (FIDLER & CHRISTIE 2019)

CHECKING IN WITH THE BASICS

It is easy to get caught up in the moment, especially when there are heightened emotions at play, and overlook some of the basics. Students with a PDA profile may have difficulty regarding eating, drinking and toileting. They may, like other autistic individuals, find it hard to read their own bodily signals and to respond to them in a helpful and timely manner. For some people with a PDA profile, once hunger or the need to use the toilet becomes urgent, it can trigger a stress response which leads to avoiding the very thing that would actually make them feel more physically comfortable. They are also likely to experience greater sensory sensitivities, so take care to scan the environment to see if there are any potentially agitating factors around. Some of these are harder to identify on behalf of another person, such as them being distracted by the uncomfortable sensation of a new pair of shoes or having had their fingernails recently trimmed.

ACCOMMODATING SENSORY SENSITIVITIES

PDA is an autism profile, so there will be sensory differences in PDAers that are not dissimilar to other autistic individuals. There are many resources available to provide information and support strategies for these sensitivities, so we will not be providing details of such an extensive subject here.

Autistic people may be overly sensitive (hypersensitive) or underly sensitive (hyposensitive) in any of their sensory modes. Some individuals may fluctuate between the two. It is vital to take note of an individual PDAer's sensory profile not only as part of understanding the holistic picture of them, but also in relation to making sensory accommodations as they need them.

It may be useful to remind ourselves of the areas of sensory differences:

- **Seeing:** Some autistic people may seek out certain things of interest to look at and really get lost in enjoying the detail of them, or they may find too much visual input overstimulating and prefer smooth, clean, unpatterned lines in their environment.
- **Touching:** This refers to whether and how someone can

tolerate touch. It doesn't mean all touch is equally difficult. For example, they may find light touch more agitating than deep pressure. They may prefer a warning before they are touched or may find the feel of certain fabrics or clothing labels unsettling.

- **Tasting:** It is not unusual for autistic individuals to have significant differences in their sense of taste. They may be able to detect differences between different brands of the same food that other people might not notice, and they may be sensitive to particular textures of food. Others may seek out stimulation and enjoy tasting strong flavors or even items that are not food.

- **Hearing:** Some people may be highly attuned to sound. They may be able to hear things that others would struggle to hear from the same distance, and may be sensitive to certain noises or pitches. They may find it easier to tolerate loud noises that are predictable or that they generate themselves than those from other sources. They may have difficulty discriminating between which noise to attend to and which to filter out.

- **Smelling:** There may be certain odors that are aversive and others that they seek. If there are particular sensitivities in this area that overlap with taste experiences, they can impact greatly on diet.

- **Proprioception:** This is the sense that gives us feedback about where our body is in the space around us and how parts of our body are moving in relation to others. It helps us, for example, to predict how much pressure we need to open a jar or give someone a gentle hug rather than a deeper squeeze. People who experience differences in this area may often bump into items or furniture or may find handwriting hard and tiring.

- **Vestibular:** This sense is about balance. It essentially tells us in what direction we are moving or are positioned. Those who are hypersensitive may get dizzy easily and often feel motion sickness. Those who are hyposensitive may seek out stimulation such as spinning or theme park rides.

- **Interoception:** This sense provides information and interpretation of what our body is experiencing and what that means. For instance, if we feel a racing heartbeat, not only will we be conscious of that sensation but we will be able to add an interpretation to it, such as "I've just run up the stairs" or "I'm nervous" or "I'm excited." Similarly, if we feel our stomach rumbling, not only are we able to acknowledge that sensation but also to work out answers to the questions "Am I unwell? Am I anxious? Am I hungry?" This sense monitors all of our visceral systems like our heart, lungs, stomach, bladder and muscles. If this sense operates in a muddled way it can have a big impact on overall wellbeing, physical health and emotional awareness.

USING FLEXIBLE AND INDIRECT APPROACHES

Due to the variable moods and high sensitivities of PDAers, using flexible and indirect approaches can be very helpful. Not only is this because they allow scope for reviewing and renegotiating situations but also because they provide opportunities for sharing control.

Using flexible approaches does not mean there is zero structure. A reasonable amount of structure is needed for organizational purposes as well as to promote a sense of purpose. However, for PDAers, this needs to be balanced with the perceived expectations that accompany that structure. For example, it can work well to have a broad structure which integrates choice on the part of the pupil, such as shown below.

ORGANIZATIONAL PLAN

The lesson will happen in Room 369

The room is booked from 10.00 to 11.30

The session will be staffed by Mrs. Mendez. Mr. Rogers will be in Room 370

Equipment that may be required for the session is stored in the staff cabinet

When the session finishes the playground will be available

Please support Brandon to choose between spending time on:

Dinosaur project	Construction kit	Science experiment
Tick if chosen	Tick if chosen	Tick if chosen
Brandon, please tell us how it went.		
Is there anything to think about for another day?		

A system like this has an overall structure but allows Brandon to choose what to fill the gaps with, including his feedback on today's session as well as thoughts for another day.

Other ways to present suggestions or requests in an indirect manner include the following:

- Framing a task as a requirement of a third-party system or policy that applies equally to both the adults and the students. For example, health and safety policies say we have to keep the fire exits free of obstacles.
- Using socially inviting language. For example, "I wonder what will happen if I try…"; "If only I knew someone who could help me with this"; "I might try learning that dance move."
- Using declarative language. This is language that shares a view or piece of information, inviting a response but not requiring one. For example, "I think using tape could fix that together"; "I really enjoyed going to the beach"; "I see your shoes are near the stairs."
- Thinking out loud. This can provide an invitational way to include a contribution to the debate or conversation. It can also offer a narrative or commentary about emotions. For example, "I was worried about starting this activity because I thought it would be too hard/boring/annoying but actually it's been fun. I will try to remember today when I think of doing this again."

OFFERING CHOICE, BUT NOT TOO MUCH CHOICE

Uncertainty and loss of agency is anxiety-provoking. Having control over our environment is soothing. When we are anxious or over-processing, having options and influence calms our systems. Our aim in supporting a PDA person is to calm their nervous systems so that they are in the best position to engage with social and learning opportunities. But there is a sweet spot between having the ability to make choices and being presented with too many choices. If we have too many choices to make, we can easily become overloaded and are then actually unable to make any choice at all. Companies know this and they build their brands upon it, so that when we go down the cereal aisle in a store, we can quickly become overwhelmed by the number of options available. We tend to select the brands we recognize on the shelves that are in our eye-line; however, we also like the illusion of having a wide choice even though we tend to select the same few items year after year!

It is beneficial to offer some choice, but there are a couple of mitigations here. First, remember that the supporting adults still retain influence over which choices are offered. We are not suggesting there are no limits or that anything and everything is available. Second, we need to determine an appropriate number of options for a PDA individual so that they feel soothed by having influence over their circumstances, without becoming overwhelmed by the extent of choices. Generally, it can be helpful to offer up to three choices, depending on the situation and the individual. It is also important that all options are positive, beneficial and totally available. That way, there is no "bad choice" to be made.

It is also crucial that a PDAer understands the different choices they are being offered and recognizes some contingencies around choice, such as "If I choose A then B is no longer available." Equally, they will need help to make informed choices, so if one option includes something they are unfamiliar with, that will need explaining as required.

When we use invitational approaches we can hang onto an adult-led priority (such as the need to wear shoes to walk down the street) but can wrap layers of invitation around it (such as "Do you want to wear sneakers or flip-flops? Do you want to put your shoes on in the kitchen or on the stairs?").

There are many flexible ways of retaining elements of control within limited choices that can reduce the perception of an expectation. For instance, James, an adult with a PDA profile, goes to a restaurant where he will often order the vegetarian sandwich and then ask them to add pastrami and ham, in preference to ordering the "mega meat treat" as prescribed on the menu.

PROVIDING PROCESSING TIME

It is commonly recognized that autistic people benefit from additional processing time. Typically this may be because they are processing a huge amount of data, including what is being asked of them, the details of what is going on around them, their social and emotional landscape, and their sensory sensitivities. Tolerating a range of demands and expectations plus managing their anxiety or elements of uncertainty adds potentially exhausting amounts of processing on a regular basis. Cameron, an adult who has a diagnosis of autism and identifies with a PDA profile, comments, "It helps me to have more time to process what you have just said or what has just happened. I don't need you to nag or to patronize me, just don't rush me."

Emma, mom to William, a 16-year-old PDAer, said, "I've learned that it helps him if I drop the seed of an idea into a conversation and just let it settle. It is most probably initially greeted with a 'No,' but some time later, it often grows into a 'Maybe.'"

In either a classroom or a home environment, it can be helpful to incorporate regular breaks for "regrouping." A PDA child may respond well to using this time to do a regulating activity to calm their sensory system, and it may be worth considering dedicating a space that is low-arousal for them to use.

In addition to providing extra processing time for PDAers, it can be highly beneficial for their supporting adults to have more time as they are also likely to be juggling lots of changing variables. We tend to make better decisions if we have a little more time to think through our options, to try to predict outcomes and to regulate ourselves. For instance, we will be more successful at keeping our "dials" synchronized if we are making careful, regulated decisions.

USING HUMOR AND ROLE PLAY

Before you try humor with a young person you will do well to get to know them first. Build rapport with them and find out what sort of humor they enjoy. Be aware of their interests and how you may incorporate them into a playful approach. They may like word play or more slapstick humor, or they may enjoy acting out scenarios with ridiculous voices for puppets or animals, and you can use these strategies to engage, to connect, to distract and move on from a tense situation as well as to teach through play. For example, pretending that a Pokémon character is whispering deliberately wrong answers to a work task from inside the child's pencil case might diffuse tension.

Many, though not all, PDAers enjoy role play. This can be used to enhance engagement or to model and try out various social situations. Some will feel more able to cooperate with demands if they are "in role" as someone else and it can be fun to go along with this to a degree. What needs to be kept in mind, however, is that the child should be encouraged to remain connected with their authentic self and not become swept away with acting as another character. Losing sight of their "real" self can have a negative impact on their self-awareness and emotional wellbeing.

BOUNDARIES

We have spoken at length in this book about being person-centered and flexible. This is indeed at the core of our approaches. However, it doesn't mean to say that there should be no boundaries. Having some boundaries can provide a sense of security as well as being more workable for families and schools. Of course, having too many rules and unnecessary boundaries can lead to children and their supporting adults getting boxed into a corner with no positive exit, which only exacerbates anxiety-driven demand avoidance and can lead to conflict.

The key is to have enough boundaries to keep everyone safe and to promote a sense of security without squandering precious time and energy on those which matter less. You can see where this overlaps with synchronizing dials as well as in relation to setting priorities.

If a student is new to your setting or service you may find it more helpful to start with very few boundaries, such as:

1. Everyone needs to be kept safe. That includes not hurting yourself or others.
2. Adults need to know where the students are at all times.

Any additional ground rules about arrival times, completed work, lining up, being responsible for their own belongings and so on can wait until further down the line, if at all.

REDUCING, BUT NOT REMOVING, ALL DEMANDS

However important it is to calibrate the dials for a PDA person so that the demands they experience do not outstrip their capacity, it is not realistic or beneficial to remove all expectations from their lives. There certainly may be periods of time when demands need to be extremely low and they will need the balance of their dials adjusting in an ongoing way, but low demand is not the same as no demand. It is about looking carefully at which expectations are reasonable, are in the individual's best interests, take account of those they are close to, will prepare them for the next steps as they mature and will support them to develop resilience. The answers to these points are going to be as varied as are the individuals concerned.

Life is scattered with expectations that will be perceived as demands by PDA individuals in different ways. For example, an expectation to eat and drink regularly is going to be perceived very differently by someone who has issues with their interoception, high anxiety and hypersensitivities in their sense of taste and smell, compared to someone else who doesn't have these experiences. Demands are not only about doing the things many children resist, like homework, chores and going to bed on time. We want to protect key relationships for PDAers, so having some reasonable expectations regarding how they interact with their friends and family will be in their long-term best interests.

According to the PDA Society, "The idea that reducing all demands or removing all boundaries is the answer to everything is erroneous. In short, the key is to reduce the 'perception' of demands and to provide a sense of control and autonomy" (PDA Society 2022).

In 2020, the author and psychiatrist Dan Siegel wrote about what he described as the "window of tolerance." Much of the work around engagement and emotional regulation since then refers to this notion. It focuses on achieving a state of optimal engagement and arousal levels. If we are either hyper-aroused or hypo-aroused we limit our ability to coordinate our processing, and our responses become more reactive and dysregulated. Many PDAers, as well as other young people who have additional needs or who have experienced trauma, may be hyper-responsive to their environment. This can get in the way of them learning and interacting, and can have a negative impact on their wellbeing. If we can identify and maximize times when their window of tolerance is most open, and also support them to have more regular capacity in their window space, they will be better able to tolerate the twists and turns of everyday life.

The "perception of demands" can be reduced in various ways, such as being indirect, and using declarative language and invitational approaches. We can also split a task. It may appeal to a young person to organize tasks as a project to be managed by them. That may be presented as them being CEO or "project manager" and their supporting adults being part of the team who are set roles by them. If the task is to complete a science experiment, they may delegate the adult to gather the equipment required and read aloud the instructions while they carry out the experiment. The adult may write the findings while the child dictates what needs to be recorded. The important elements here are that the child has engaged with the activity, is participating in learning and the adult has recorded the conclusions the child has come to.

In terms of other everyday activities, splitting and delegating tasks can be a good way to help children and teenagers tidy their rooms, make a snack, feed the dog, and so on.

Another helpful way to view repeating tasks like brushing teeth, bathing and wearing clean clothes is to view them in categories of possibility. You may want to create your own categories, such as tasks that are everyday (drinking and eating, interacting, getting out of bed), most days (brushing teeth, changing clothes), once a week (putting toys away, washing hair), and only when possible days (going to the store/movies/grandparents' house).

PROVIDING RECOVERY TIME

It is easy for PDA individuals to get overstimulated and overwhelmed by lots of demands or big experiences. These may not necessarily be negative; they may include birthdays or holidays that have been enjoyable at the time but which have also been emotionally costly. Even if a PDAer appears to be coping, we should remain conscious that they may be masking or placing untenable pressure on themselves to contain what they are experiencing.

Sometimes, everyday life can feel relentless for many of us, especially with the pressures of working, childcare, running a household and paying bills. Children have their own pressures too. For those who are trying to sustain school attendance there are very particular challenges. Whether their day went beautifully or dreadfully, there is an ongoing expectation of attendance and compliance the day after, and the day after that, and the day after that...

Ideally, PDAers will develop their own awareness of when they are reaching their threshold of tolerance and be able to voice this to take a break. However, that is not always possible. It may be because they are still young and their self-awareness is not at that level yet, or because there are issues in their emotional regulation so they can feel taken by surprise by their own feelings, or they may be working really hard to "hold it together" because they want to do well and don't want to upset or disappoint anyone. Maybe they don't know that taking a break is even an option.

As mature adults, where feasible, we try to build in time to regulate and to regain our peace of mind. If we know that we have had a very busy period at work, we may book a vacation day or organize a quiet weekend to recover. We need to make similar accommodations for our young PDAers. On a day-to-day basis that may look like them having some quiet time to themselves after school, or if they are homeschooled it may be helpful to incorporate regular break periods during the day when they can access their regulating activities. If there is a particularly big event such as a school trip, family celebration or appointment, it can be beneficial to consider what support will help, not only during the event, but also before and afterwards.

Some of the preparation beforehand may include helping them understand what is likely to happen at the event and how it may feel for them. Some of them will need time to process a big experience and to regain their equilibrium before they are ready to return to "business as usual." Adult PDAer Julia Daunt talks about this and has created what she calls her "demand regulation cycle." What this represents is a cycle of needing to prepare for an activity, accounting for energies required to carry out the activity and allowing herself some recovery time post-event. She also notes that some events need more recovery time than others depending on how well they have gone and what reserves she has needed to use up. It is an interesting model to consider for children, teenagers and young adults with PDA profiles, and it can be good to involve them in creating their own demand regulation cycle (see Figure 4.2).

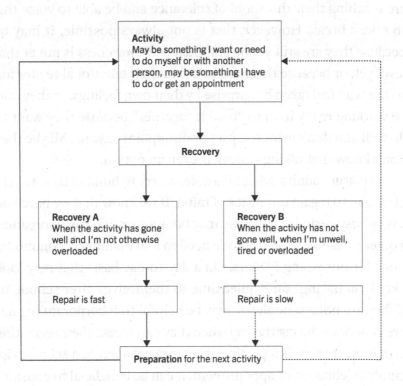

FIGURE 4.2 DEMAND REGULATION CYCLE (FIDLER & DAUNT 2021)

PRAISE, REWARDS AND CONSEQUENCES

Adults use praise, rewards and consequences as typical ways of encouraging children to use wanted behaviors and discouraging them from using unwanted behaviors. When used in moderation and with kindness, these conventional strategies continue to be popular across society. However, they rely on a few key skills and fundamental assumptions. Among the assumptions are that children should conform to the "accepted" balance of power between themselves and adults, and that children who are unable to comply are viewed as "poorly behaved," which prompts adults to increase their rigid and punitive responses.

It is an often-quoted phrase, originally said by a parent of her PDA daughter, that she "can't help won't." What she meant was that, at certain times, her daughter wouldn't do things, but that she couldn't help the fact that she wouldn't in that moment.

The reasons that conventional behavioral strategies work for many neurotypical children is that, generally speaking, they are better able to manage their impulses, to understand their emotions and to predict consequences, are motivated to avoid shame or regret, and are also motivated to prioritize a delayed reward over a current aversive experience (e.g. tidy your bedroom/finish your homework, then we can watch a movie/go to the park). PDA individuals have differences in their self-awareness, emotional understanding, anxiety, social relationships and sensory sensitivities. We see how much less effective conventional approaches to rewards and consequences are for very young children who have yet to develop in these areas, so really, we ought not to be surprised that others, who have also not refined the necessary skills, do not respond well either.

Raelene Dundon notes in her book *PDA in the Therapy Room*:

> For children with PDA, their demand avoidance is not a conscious choice but is an adaptive response to feeling threatened, and as such is not fully in the child's control. Consequently, rewarding compliance and employing negative consequences when the child is defiant is ineffective and only serves to cause the child more distress as they are unable to achieve success. (Dundon 2021)

Alan, a dad, commented:

> We can have lengthy discussions about how it would be beneficial
> for them to behave. In spite of them agreeing to do/not do some-
> thing, sometimes even the best reward you could imagine wouldn't
> be enough to help them get over the block of what they see as an
> intolerable demand at that moment.

Steph, mother to Sasha, writes:

> Trying to impose any kind of consequence for not doing work was
> pointless as it would lead to extreme, distressed meltdowns that
> could take hours to pass. Consequences didn't lead to any learning,
> and they didn't teach her any skills to be able to cope with the
> initial demands. (Curtis 2024)

We want to teach children, teenagers and young adults about the
benefits of being kind, respectful and generous-spirited toward
others; it's just that learning these principles is not likely to happen
by punishing them for making mistakes. Natural consequences can
be helpful to teach outcomes in a way that is less direct and nonjudgmental, and that hopefully leads the child to draw some of their
own conclusions. For instance, it might present an opportunity for
a useful conversation if the child's request to go on a bike ride is not
possible today because the bikes are locked in the garage, the child
threw the garage key over the yard wall yesterday, and it hasn't been
found, rather than being scolded for having done so in the first place.

Rewards can be complicated for PDAers too. For some, who tend
to be perfectionists, the pressure of doing something to an excellent standard can be overwhelming. For those who feel discomfort
under social scrutiny, being seen to complete a task that is linked to
the reward can feel like an insurmountable barrier. For those who
are highly sensitive to demands, no reward is going to override the
anxiety that is triggered by the expectation. Reward systems that

require sustained cooperation can be destined to fail because they don't allow for variable sensitivities to demands. Working toward a reward at the end of a week, or even the end of a day, may simply be too far away.

All this is to say that the pressures that accompany praise or rewards can have an enormously negative impact on PDA individuals.

We still want to encourage PDAers and to give them rewarding experiences for doing well. Having a surprise bonus or an unanticipated upgrade can work well for children with a PDA profile. That way, they have the pleasure of the "reward" but without the pressure. If it's a joint reward, so that there is less focus on the individual, it is less direct: for example, "I reckon we've done really well with that job today. I think we deserve a treat. Should we go to the beach or the mall?"

PERSONALIZING THE CURRICULUM

For a student with a PDA profile to learn and to thrive, we need to look carefully *what* we teach them. Academic subjects have their role to play, especially where they overlap with personal interests and employment opportunities, but what is most important is learning that prepares for adulthood such as problem-solving, social relationships, organizing time and equipment for a task, self-awareness, understanding emotions, self-care, accessing a community, and so on.

Schools will have their own curriculum requirements, some of which are less flexible, but to truly meet the needs of their students with a PDA profile, they will need to think outside the box. There are more suggestions in this regard in Chapter 7 about creating a framework.

A learning plan created by a multidisciplinary team to support emotional regulation and engagement might include some of the elements shown below.

LEARNING PLAN

Learning intention	Approaches to be used	Facilitated by who	Evidence of progress toward learning intention (see lesson notes for details)	Next review
To engage in guided sensory experiences that focus on mindful awareness and improve interoception	To use naturally arising opportunities to describe touching and tasting foods, using preferred food	Mom Teacher Therapist	Described touching ice as cold, smooth and calming Expressed preferences of different sweet, salty and sour candies	
To explore feelings through drawing, creating comic strips or story-writing with a focus on what might have caused or contributed to an emotional reaction	Starting with feelings that are already familiar, e.g. hungry or tired, and working toward including emotions, especially where they may be linked to feelings, e.g. I couldn't cope with that because I was too tired	Mom Teacher Therapist	Engaged in drawing a comic strip using speech and thought bubbles to demonstrate what a character was feeling and thinking Demonstrated awareness of sensation being linked to feeling an emotion, e.g. feeling anxious in noisy environments	End of semester
To learn and use key emotional vocabulary regarding a range of everyday emotions	To use emotional vocabulary such as happy, sad, mad, scared To learn emotional vocabulary that refers to degrees of feeling such as irritated, frustrated	Mom Teacher Therapist	Used sad, happy and scared appropriately to describe previous experiences Uses some of own preferred terms, e.g. "buzzing for real" when happy about something	End of semester
To recognize own characteristics	Starting with physical characteristics to also include personality traits and preferences	Mom Teacher Therapist	Aware of physical differences from siblings/friends Recognizes own skills in sports	End of semester
To be involved in own learning about subjects of personal interests	To guide content and pace of personalized learning	Mom Teacher Therapist	Visited science lab to observe lesson Watched similar experiments online	End of semester

AUTONOMOUS LEARNING

For various reasons already explored, PDA individuals may encounter a series of challenges regarding engaging with learning activities that others "present" to them, especially where there are additional elements of pressure and expectation, such as organized lessons, written work to complete or tests to study for. "Teaching," wherever that happens, is more likely to be successful if it is based on personal interests and is facilitated by a supporting adult, not "dispensed" to the student. As with other activities, it will be helpful where there can be autonomy. According to Fidler and Christie (2019), "Involving the young person in the process of planning their curriculum can in itself reduce anxiety about loss of control and avoids them seeing the curriculum as something that is being 'imposed' on them."

Autonomous learning means that learning is led by the child, not by the adult or a prescribed curriculum. Topics of study can be identified by the learner, and the role of the supporting adult is to provide guidance, resources and encouragement that enable the learner to make the next steps and enrich their own learning. Being an autonomous learner should also give you access to discussions about where, how and with whom you would like to learn. It moves the emphasis away from something that happens "to" a child, teenager or young adult, and toward something that happens "with" them. A key starting point in these discussions is to explore interests together and see what learning opportunities could link naturally. Planning through interests can help strengthen learning and embed person-centered approaches. A downloadable copy of the form below is available for families or professionals to complete.

PLANNING FOR LEARNING THROUGH INTERESTS

Oakley is interested in	Oakley's comments about this subject	Potential areas of learning related to this interest
Cycling	Cycling is better on a windy day so I can feel the breeze on my face. Cycling is good when I get "bored legs" because it gives them a good workout. I like to sing out loud when I cycle. I like to have a cycle-buddy when I'm in the mood: it's easier to talk to someone while we cycle than if we're sitting down	Health and fitness Mechanics Route planning Road safety Cycling playlist selections Nutrition Social opportunities for cycling buddies Cycle machine indoors with fan blowing as bad weather alternative. Could cycle generate energy to power the fan?
Manga	Manga is so cool. My friend Eva is really good at drawing Manga characters. I want to get as good as her one day. Eva says we could make our own comic. I'm getting more interested in Japan. I might even like to go and visit when I'm older	History of art Japanese culture Learning Japanese language Imaginative story-writing Creating characters, developing self-awareness and understanding social relationships
Cooking	Cooking is relaxing for me. It's a great way of eating my favorite food that I can make just how I like. I like making snacks for my family to have on movie nights. My friends like it when I make cookies and I like trying out new flavors with them. I would like to prepare a three-course meal one day, but I would need a sous chef	Math concepts Organizing materials for a task and following instructions (a recipe) Creativity in adapting/personalizing recipes Potential work experience or social enterprise Social opportunities in cooking for friends or family. Artistic opportunities re table decorations or making invitations Geography/history curriculum re recipes from different countries or through time. Recipes that reflect different eras, social groups, available ingredients, religious or holiday specialities Using different cooking utensils and electrical appliances Growing fruit and vegetables for ingredients Science learning re reactions between ingredients and flavor blending Shopping for goods Budgeting

Marty, at the age of 14, developed an interest in military history which grew out of conversations with his grandfather who was a veteran. He began to create a film archive of interviews not only with his grandpa but also some of his grandpa's friends. At this time, Marty was not attending school. In fact, he had stopped attending by the time he finished elementary school due to his anxiety and autistic burnout. Marty had a tutor, called Leo, as part of his home education program who facilitated his autonomous learning in history and film making. By the age of 17 he was giving talks at his local history society, accompanied by his grandpa. Leo was instrumental in encouraging Marty and guiding him to access next steps, as and when he was ready. Marty hasn't returned to school but has a driver's license, has learned to cook a small range of meals for the family, does some voluntary work in his local library and is considering a college course in the future.

There are undoubtedly a number of challenges in facilitating learning for children, teenagers and young adults with a PDA profile. Some of the contributory factors include a late diagnosis, a missing diagnosis or a misdiagnosis, which can lead to needs not being recognized. There are other challenges that are integral to the American school system, which will be explored in Chapter 6. What we hope families can hang onto is that things change, not only at national levels (although progress in this area can be painfully slow), but also in the development of young PDAers. Ethan's mum said when her son was 13:

> I can't wait for him to be an adult. He will be so much of a better adult than he knows how to be a child. People minimize the voices of children and he finds that so frustrating, but no one thinks it's unreasonable for adults to have more control over their lives than children. He has aspirations and he's smart. He wants to work and have a good adult life and I'm sure he will.

Ethan is now in his 20s, working as an engineer, has a satisfying social life, is considering continuing his college studies and is in the process of buying his first home.

Julia, who has just turned 40, had a very mixed experience of education. She left high school without qualifications despite having achieved good grades in her lessons. She reflects:

> It seems a bit strange that after those [test] results I don't have any formal qualifications to my name, but I don't mind... I know that I have got a good brain and that I'm clever... I don't feel that having certificates defines me... I don't need them for the life I now lead. (Fidler & Daunt 2021)

Julia now works as a self-employed trainer for the PDA Society, has a number of commitments to nonprofit organizations, and lives with her partner of almost 20 years.

It is impossible to know what lies ahead for children who are not yet adults, but there is every reason to remain optimistic and aspirational.

CHAPTER 5

PROMOTING EMOTIONAL WELLBEING

In the context of our understanding of PDA as an anxiety-driven need to control and to avoid everyday expectations, combined with a hypersensitivity to those expectations, a significant part of any support will involve looking closely at promoting emotional wellbeing. In practice, this is not only the emotional wellbeing of the children and young people with a PDA profile but also of those who live and work with them.

Research literature has identified factors that universally contribute to stress as those that represent uncertainty, lack of information and loss of control (Levine & Ursin 1978). It is not hard to imagine how all these elements could apply to PDA individuals and their families.

A helpful starting point when considering emotional wellbeing can be to consider what we mean by the term. For instance, let's consider the World Health Organization (WHO) definition of mental health:

> The WHO constitution states: "Health is a state of complete physical, mental and social well-being and not merely the absence of disease or infirmity." An important implication of this definition is that mental health is more than just the absence of mental disorders or disabilities.

Mental health is a state of well-being in which an individual realizes his or her own abilities, can cope with the normal stresses of life, can work productively and is able to make a contribution to his or her community.

Mental health is fundamental to our collective and individual ability as humans to think, emote, interact with each other, earn a living and enjoy life. On this basis, the promotion, protection and restoration of mental health can be regarded as a vital concern of individuals, communities and societies throughout the world. (World Health Organization 2023)

Although there are troubling statistics about the prevalence of poor mental health in autistic individuals, being autistic does not necessarily lead to mental health issues. It is not having one's autism understood, or in the case of PDAers often not even having it recognized, plus not having one's needs met, that contributes to the difficulties. This is because, quite simply, under these circumstances the load on an individual exceeds their capacity. We need to equip our young people with self-knowledge, the means to communicate and the resilience to cope with the stress, disappointment and sadness that, unfortunately, ordinary life may bring to any of us. There are times when something occurs internally or externally that causes us raised anxiety, stress or exhaustion. Where this starts to become clinically significant lies in looking at the impact it has on the individual and their ability to manage their life in the way they had been previously accustomed to, or in such a way that impedes their ability to thrive.

When we talk about increasing a PDAer's tolerance to stress, disappointment or sadness, to be clear, we are not talking about expecting them to think or behave as though they didn't have a PDA profile, nor are we asking them to tolerate something unreasonable. We want to equip them for an adult life where they are enabled to speak for themselves, to explore new opportunities and to enjoy relationships and hobbies that work for them. If any of us were to avoid all potentially anxiety-provoking experiences where we don't have full control, such as starting a new relationship, getting a job, moving homes, going on a trip or trying a new restaurant, we could quickly find our opportunities for a full, satisfying and interesting life curtailed. What we want to promote in young people is resilience, so that with support, they are able to accommodate setbacks.

When things are going well for PDAers we need to pay attention to what contributes to that, as closely as we do when things are going less well. We need to be conscious of what we are doing that is working, of how we are doing it, who is instrumental in delivering it and how we can sustain it. Becoming complacent about any of these aspects will soon remind us that progress can be sensitive and fragile so needs constantly revisiting.

There are two important elements to promoting emotional well-being. One focuses on proactive work to try to prevent an individual becoming overwhelmed in the first place, and this should consume the bulk of our endeavors. Over time we will be aiming for the young person to understand themselves well enough and develop their own coping strategies so that they are an active partner in the proactive process. The other element is reactive, that is, how to respond when the person we support has reached their tipping point into overload. There is a place for both elements, although obviously we hope that by putting more work into proactive approaches, we will need fewer reactive ones. Achieving sustainable, proactive approaches will not only be good for the young person themselves but also for those living and working with them.

GETTING THE BASICS RIGHT

There are a number of anxiety-reducing approaches that help lots of autistic individuals. Many of these center around reducing uncertainty by providing structure, routine and clear expectations. For reasons that have already been described, these approaches tend not to work well for PDAers, because while on the one hand they reduce unpredictability, on the other they are loaded with demands and expectations. That doesn't mean that none of these approaches are useful. Again, it comes back to understanding the individual so as to personalize their support. As outlined in Chapter 4, there are ways of presenting a degree of structure infused with flexible options which may better suit a child with a PDA profile. It will be better to reduce uncertainty by offering additional information, options and a flexible time scale.

There are other basics that can be helpful and should not be overlooked that may reduce the likelihood of stress or overload, such as making appropriate sensory accommodations, getting restorative sleep, good nutrition and self-care.

Exercise is not only physically but also mentally beneficial. You will need to determine what suits the individual best. If a young person has spent a significant amount of time in the home because they have withdrawn from many everyday activities, particularly those outside their home, you may need to begin with something very low-key that is easy to adapt, such as a short walk. Being out in a natural environment, in a way that works for the individual's sensitivities, can carry huge benefits in terms of mental health, fitness, digestion and reducing stress. It may also be a way to connect with others or develop an interest. Walking alongside may provide a more neutral forum for having conversations compared to having a face-to-face interaction.

MINDFULNESS

Mindful activities such as yoga encourage those who practice it to focus on their experience of the present. When we focus on the present, we concentrate on what is happening right now and we stop ruminating on what has gone before or imagining what may come after. We stop interpreting and try to settle with what we feel. The poses in yoga practice are useful to guide us to do this, because for most of us it is too challenging to sustain mindful awareness without a physical prompt to ground us. There are of course other activities that can achieve the same process, but we use yoga as an example because it is well known.

A benefit of yoga for emotional wellbeing is that it encourages us to acknowledge a tolerable degree of physical discomfort without overprocessing it, simply to notice it but not to overreact to it. Over time, activities that can teach us to be less hyper-responsive to alerting stimuli can quieten our responses to everyday stresses and irritants. To clarify, we are not suggesting that we want to coach our youngsters to accept unreasonable or unsustainable amounts of pain or distress; this is about reframing responses to manageable amounts of these experiences.

Children and young people may also like to explore mindful practice while they are doing something that creates a notable sensation, such as letting chocolate melt slowly in their mouths. This kind of input will also support their developing interoception by increasing awareness of bodily sensations.

FLOW

"Flow" refers to experiencing a sense of flow within an activity—the sort of moments when we "lose ourselves" in a positive way. Some people feel like this when exercising, playing a musical instrument, dancing or making artwork. It is characterized by doing something that demands our attention so that, as Mihaly Csikszentmihalyi describes it, "there is no energy left over to process any information but what the activity offers us." He continues:

As a result, one of the most universal and distinctive features of optimal experience takes place: people become so involved in what they are doing that the activity becomes spontaneous, almost automatic; they stop being aware of themselves as separate from the actions they are performing. (Csikszentmihalyi 1990)

Flow is different from mindfulness in so far as, when we are mindful, we are aware of ourselves and we are learning to be with ourselves. Flow can give us a break from our thinking selves. Devising a beneficial combination of both mindfulness and flow will look different from one person to another. Many autistic people may be able to find experiences of flow through their special interests. These moments can be calming and nurturing. However, it is worth taking account of the nature of those special interests, because, in some cases, there may be a developing fascination with something negative, violent or otherwise harmful, either to themselves or to others, which will need to be managed sensitively. There may be situations where the topic of a special interest is troubling, such as violent crime or weaponry. There may be other examples where although the young person is expressing that their chosen activity provides them with motivation and satisfaction, it is having some detrimental side effects. This may happen with activities such as gaming. Gaming is an extremely popular and enjoyable pastime, but it is also designed to be addictive. If a young person's mental health is in a particularly fragile place, there might be a valid rationale for not encouraging them to limit their gaming at a given point in time. However, as with other activities that affect our lives, if it is starting to interfere with opportunities for engagement with learning, social relationships, physical health, sleep patterns and mental health, the supporting adults have a duty of care to that person's wellbeing and will need to have some carefully considered, individualized conversations about a balanced approach. In the majority of cases, though, we would anticipate special interests to be positive, and having regular access to experiences of flow will help concentration, learning and regulation.

FINDING A HAPPY PLACE

Some PDA individuals may feel at their most peaceful when they are outdoors, by the ocean or with animals. The options are as varied as the individuals. Everyone does better if they have a place of sanctuary where they are accepted and supported by a warm loving network. For most but not all children, that place is at home with their family. We need to acknowledge this for PDAers who find school attendance particularly challenging, and we need to listen with an open mind about why coming to school is so difficult for them.

We need to consider how we can provide at least some aspect of a student's school experience that represents a happy place. In doing so it will help to think about a student's sensory sensitivities, their personal interests and activities that regulate them.

LIGHTENING THE LOAD

Children with a PDA profile typically carry a heavier load of anxiety than most. This means that so do their families and supporting adults, so this key point applies to many of you reading this.

Every day, we carry an emotional load with us, but there are some days when that load feels lighter than others. It is not necessarily true that we actually carry less on those days, but something is different that can help the load feel less burdensome. If you imagine your emotional luggage being carried in a suitcase, some days we feel like we are dragging an unwieldy heavy leather case everywhere we go. Other times it might feel like a modern lightweight case with wheels and a handle adjusted perfectly to our height. On our best day, our case may be metaphorically on a luggage trolley with room for snacks and a takeaway drink.

Children and young people with a PDA profile may need just such a variety of methods of moving their emotional luggage around. If they can be encouraged to identify what helps them on a good day and what hinders them on a tough day, they can be active contributors to looking after their emotional wellbeing. When children are very young, their carers need to do a lot of this work for them. As they mature, we want this process to be shared as they edge to a place where they are able to take a more active part in their own wellbeing. That is not to say that the supporting adults are no longer willing or available to help them, but it is important that young people gain confidence and capacity to spot early warning signals so they can put personal interventions into action for themselves.

SUPPORTING CHILDREN WHO MASK

There has been increasing awareness of how often and how many autistic individuals mask or camouflage their differences. This seems to particularly be a feature of autistic girls, PDAers and undiagnosed or late-diagnosed people who are driven to "fit in" and who have been historically conscious of their differences, without understanding why they feel different. They are motivated to do well and seek to appear to do well. "Doing well" may be interpreted as doing "the same as the majority of others," or certainly the appearance of what others seem to have, to look like or appear to be doing. Social media has not been helpful in this regard for many of our young people.

What will benefit PDAers, as with other autistic youngsters, is for them to connect with and to accept their authentic selves. The pressures of masking can be exhausting and will in the end take an emotional toll on wellbeing and ultimately health. In this regard we can promote good mental health by working with them, at their own pace, on matters of self-awareness, emotional literacy and regulation.

Having said all that, it should also be noted that there are moments when a certain (manageable and small) amount of camouflaging our true feelings in everyday life can have its uses. For example, it may be refreshingly honest, but not always advisable, to tell your work colleagues exactly what you think of them (unless there is a malpractice issue to raise of course). It is not the case that all honesty is good, and all masking is bad. It is not a binary issue, and that's what makes it complicated. The key is to understand how much, how often, in front of who and for what reason we are masking, and to balance that with times when we are able to do the activities that regulate us, to share our authentic selves within close relationships and, crucially, to accept ourselves for who we are with all our attributes. Recognizing the subtle nuances of getting this balance right is not a straightforward process and requires constant review.

Julia Daunt writes:

> Masking helps me to bring out my smoothest social skills. Without it I would be too nervous to socialise and I would worry about coming across negatively or too childishly. As long as I don't have to mask for too long or too often, it actually serves a useful purpose. (Fidler & Daunt 2021)

Having said that, masking is exhausting and uncomfortable, and no autistic person should have to feel they need to conceal their autism. Helping autistic youngsters to understand the best way for them to navigate this will require time to specifically explore issues regarding context and improve their understanding of potential consequences, both to themselves and to others, so that as they enhance their self-awareness and self-worth they are protected from paying a high price in their emotional wellbeing.

IMPROVING INTEROCEPTION

Our recent understanding of interoception has been extended from theory to practical application by the work of Kelly Mahler.

Kelly has developed a suite of teaching tools to support young people's learning in this area, including a curriculum (see www.kelly-mahler.com).

As discussed in Chapter 4, interoception refers to our ability to recognize the physical sensations we are experiencing and then to interpret these feelings. If we can make sense of our physical sensations, that can also lead us to solutions such as "If my stomach is growling and I'm feeling lightheaded it might mean I'm hungry, so I will feel better if I eat something. Okay, time to get a snack." Interoception is a cornerstone in achieving self-regulation. As part of their autism profile, PDAers may experience differences in their interoception.

We can support children and young people with their interoception using an individualized combination of approaches. It might be helpful to try the following:

- Increasing awareness of sensory experiences by focusing on the physical feeling of touching an item or looking at the detail of an object. It is important with this kind of work that we take account of any sensory sensitivities so as not to cause aversive reactions. It is also important not to contribute to overprocessing of sensory input in such a way that could invite new intolerances to stimuli. It might be most helpful to do this work in a pulsing manner, that is, to step into the sensation and back from the sensation at intervals. Children with a PDA profile may resist planned or guided sessions, so it may be better for the supporting adult to keep the strategies in mind and introduce them as opportunities naturally arise, such as eating an ice cream in the park, having a bath, cooking, or playing in the sandbox.
- Using strategies such as the 5, 4, 3, 2, 1 grounding technique. This is where you identify five things you can see, four that you can touch, three that you can hear, two that you can smell and one that you can taste. There are benefits in this

technique regarding grounding in the present moment as well as connecting with sensory input.

- Regular access to activities that are known to soothe, especially sensory activities, working toward recognizing the impact of these and being able to implement them increasingly independently.
- Recognition of the physical sensations associated with raised emotion in themselves, such as sweating palms, increased heart rate, and awareness of linking these to emotional vocabulary or associated feelings. Extending this work over time could incorporate identifying degrees of emotion and recognizing more than one emotion about the same event or situation.
- Slow deliberate movements, which can increase awareness of physical sensations and position, especially movements that stretch our muscles, require that we balance, or carry something heavy.

Improving interoceptive awareness can also play a key role in helping young people to spot the early warning signals that indicate dysregulation. The more effectively they can do this the better they will be at preventing a tip into overload. For children who are at the early stages of developing this awareness, it is up to the adults around them to look for the early warning signals. Inevitably sometimes they are missed, or as often happens for PDAers, the change occurs too quickly to have time to intervene. As children get older it becomes increasingly important that they are active in self-regulation. Equally, it is important that as supporting adults we recognize our own regulation. We are, of course, subject to our own mood fluctuations, and when we spend time with someone who is dysregulated and anxious it can have an impact on us too. The better regulated the adults are, the better we will be able to help the children we support; therefore doing some of this work in tandem can benefit adults as well as children.

PROMOTING EMOTIONAL INTELLIGENCE

The term "emotional intelligence," often associated with the work of Goleman (Goleman 1996, 1998), refers to understanding our own emotions, our ability to articulate our feelings and how we manage them in relation to others. It includes our ability to recognize the causes of emotions and to appreciate the emotions of others as well as how we integrate that understanding into our social relationships. The art of understanding our emotional landscape, soothing our fluctuating moods and managing interpersonal relationships can be an exhausting and complex task, particularly for PDAers.

Madison, aged 16, said, "When I was younger, it's not only that I didn't realize that what I felt every day was called anxiety, but I didn't know that everyone else didn't feel the same as me." Madison learned to recognize her emotions, connecting with them via her increased awareness of the physical sensations associated with them, like nausea and sweating. She was then able to identify them and work toward understanding what had contributed to causing them. Finally, she was able to link her awareness with what she could do to try to counteract the heightened and exhausting levels of emotional intensity she experienced.

Working on all of this is a complex and long-term learning goal. Children and young people with a PDA profile, as well as other students with additional needs, can be helped to do this work by having dedicated wellbeing times within their schedule with a trusted adult. These are sessions described as "personal tutorials" in *Collaborative Approaches to Learning for Pupils with PDA* (Fidler & Christie 2019), which offer weekly opportunities to focus on social and emotional learning, wellbeing, self-advocacy and independence. While sessions such as personal tutorials are times to reflect on previous events and interactions, it is equally important that we do not reinforce unhelpful rumination. Sometimes PDAers can hang onto a grudge or go over and over an upsetting event which starts to have a negative impact on their wellbeing. There may be some who might benefit from professional therapeutic help, alongside support from school staff and families to work through more complex issues.

It is not only negative emotions that can be difficult for children and young people with a PDA profile. Sometimes any deviation from an emotional mid-line can be very unsettling.

Brandon, aged 11, said:

I get really excited about my birthday but sometimes I get too excited, then it all goes wrong. It's best if I know what's going to be inside all my presents before I open them and if no one talks about the theme park that I like to visit. I want to go and it was my idea to ask for Mom to take us. I try not to even think about the theme park because if I think about it too much the excitement squashes the whole thing and we will have to end up cancelling.

FINDING A VOICE

As PDAers improve their self-awareness and emotional literacy, we also want to encourage them to develop self-advocacy. That is, to be able to express their views and choices in an assertive, though not confrontational, manner.

To be able to do this most effectively they will benefit from, in the first instance, being able to identify what their feelings and preferences are, and then to find a way to express them so that they can be heard. Sometimes this can be achieved in person and verbally, especially if that is to a trusted person in their lives. At other times, being asked to do so, particularly if in a wider forum such as a school meeting, may feel too demanding. If that is the case, it is paramount that adults find creative ways to let the voice of the young person be an integral feature of any planning. For example, they may feel more comfortable contributing a short video message, a dictated letter or a piece of artwork as their way of expressing their views.

Self-advocacy doesn't only mean articulating what we want but also what we don't want. Teaching PDAers a variety of ways to say no, other than using confrontation, shutdown or escape, will be extremely useful. For instance, consider the following responses when turning down a request:

- No, sorry I've changed my mind.
- No, I don't know how to do it.
- No, I don't remember how to do it.
- No, I don't really understand what you're asking me.
- No, it's too hard for me.
- No, I'm afraid something else has come up now.
- No, I can't do it just now, but can you ask me again later?
- No, I am overwhelmed by that or maybe by everything.
- No, I'm not motivated by that idea unfortunately.
- No, I can't because I'm too hungry/tired/unwell.

You may be able to add your own ideas to this list. It is not intended to be exhaustive, it is meant to illustrate the point that there are a number of valid reasons for declining something which most of us use from time to time. These responses help us have our position understood and offer explanations that reduce the risk of damage to the relationship.

ALLOWING RECOVERY TIME

As we noted in Chapter 4, Julia Daunt writes about what she describes as a demand regulation cycle. Julia's demand regulation cycle is a repeating pattern of preparing for an activity, coping with the activity, recovering from the activity, then preparing for the next. Depending on what the activity is and how well it has gone this can sometimes be a complicated and lengthy process.

Another way to facilitate recovery time may be to postpone certain tasks or arrangements even if they were previously planned and agreed. This is not to say something is cancelled permanently, but that there is a carefully considered decision to put it to one side just now. Indeed, teaching the concept of postponing rather than cancelling can be very supportive to PDA individuals, especially as they mature. Postponing can make the difference between abandoning an enjoyable activity altogether and rescheduling it. Additionally, some tasks that are not possible to continue with at this moment may also be delegated to someone who is able and willing to pick them up temporarily.

The better youngsters get at recognizing their emotional landscape and expressing it, the more this will enhance their ability to appreciate what is realistic and achievable on a given day. That means if there is a day when eating a meal and talking to other people is as much as can be managed, there is less reason to feel it has not been a good day. Don't underestimate the power of small incremental gains. There is a saying attributed to the Dalai Lama: "if you think you're too small to make a difference, try sleeping with a mosquito."

PLANNING EMERGENCY EXITS FOR EMOTIONAL WELLBEING

Most adults feel more comfortable in stressful situations if they know they can make a graceful exit should they feel the need. These exits might be subtle, such as taking a bathroom break or a breath of fresh air, or they may be more distinct, such as making excuses about childcare arrangements or a bogus phone call that needs to be made. Moreover, as adults there are far fewer situations that we find ourselves stuck in than there are for children, school classrooms being a prime example.

It is really important that we work with PDAers to develop reasonable, agreed ways for them to leave an untenably difficult situation. If we don't, we can have inadvertently contributed to them resorting to more dramatic behavior in order to do so. Working with your students with a PDA profile you can put together a system of how to access breaks, an agreed place to go to, a safe person to seek out, and a smooth way to return to class or to the social group.

These proactive approaches present a starting point, and you will need to create an individualized package comprised of a combination of elements that are relevant to the person you know.

TAKING A BREAK

Reactive responses may include a "time to take five" approach that can be implemented by the PDA individual or by those who support them. Sometimes these breaks are necessary, but when they occur in difficult circumstances, try to make them positive. Find a way of expressing, "We left there because it was no longer within a tolerable level of overload" (wouldn't we all choose to do that?). Also, celebrate when the child has been able to exit gracefully and relatively calmly rather than by actions such as breaking something, hurting someone, running away, being unkind, deliberately shocking others or being threatening to someone else.

When autistic people, including PDAers, have experienced ongoing overload and stress they may have what is sometimes referred to as an "autistic burnout." Autistic burnout has been explored by Dr. Dora Raymaker (assistant research professor at Portland State University) and the team that she co-directs at the Academic Autism Spectrum Partnership in Research and Education (AASPIRE; www.aaspire.org). Following a qualitative study to look at the skilled employment of autistic adults (Raymaker et al. 2020) an unexpected theme arose that led to further research on the theme of autistic burnout. Autistic burnout is not a new concept. The AASPIRE study developed a definition of it as "a syndrome conceptualised as resulting from chronic life stress and a mismatch of expectations and abilities without adequate support."

Autistic burnout is characterized by experiencing a pervasive, long-term (longer than three months) exhaustion, loss of function and reduced tolerance to stimuli. How this is characterized in autistic individuals is by an increase in their sensory sensitivities as well as in meltdowns/shutdowns, which are often related to their autism profile, and a decrease in executive function, cognitive skills and social communication, all combined with chronic exhaustion. In short, in an autistic burnout many things a person was managing to do previously have now become things they cannot continue doing. For some children, this is their experience of trying to sustain school attendance in a setting where their needs are not being met. Understandably, those who tend to mask at school are particularly vulnerable to it because they are working hard to camouflage the degree to which they are struggling. Again, related to their autism, they may not actually recognize or express that they are increasingly struggling until the situation overwhelms them.

In cases where a child or young person has reached this point, they may withdraw from activities they were previously doing and enjoying. Not only might that include attending school, it can in some instances even include leaving their bedroom, or they may become nocturnal. In addition, a reduction in tolerance to sensory input can make it hard for those experiencing autistic burnout to tolerate certain foods or some everyday sensations regarding self-care, or to access public spaces or social interaction. At this point, taking a break has become unavoidable.

There is discussion regarding whether this form of "burnout" or "autistic inertia" can be categorized as "autistic catatonia," whereby individuals become stuck and experience difficulty in carrying out ordinary movements. In autistic individuals this is often where there has been chronic stress and a marked deterioration in functioning. Amitta Shah, who has worked extensively in this area, has developed support that recommends a non-medical holistic approach that takes account of the person's psychological profile and their environment. She calls it the "psycho-ecological approach" (Shah 2019), and it has a lot in common with other holistic, person-centered and collaborative approaches that are described in this book.

Following just such a burnout, Rosa stopped attending school and retreated to her bedroom. She felt unable to dress, to talk, to eat with others and even to open her birthday presents, which remained waiting outside her bedroom door for many months. Over a long period of time, with professionals working closely with her loving and committed family, she found alternative ways to communicate when she was unable to talk, and slowly emerged from her room. She was helped by a series of indirect prompts which helped her initiate action without pressurizing her. Initially this was just to one other room of the house, but this eventually led to using the whole house and garden alongside others and later to joining family outings and visiting places of interest. Re-engaging with educational learning has been a more complicated and slower process but she has begun to write via her passion for reading, and this is how she is finding her voice again. She has written about what she describes as her "frozen years" and that she needed time to thaw. She loves animals and hopes to expand her learning by working with horses.

Sadly, for some individuals a lengthy period of recovery time is required. It goes without saying that prevention is better than cure, but following an autistic burnout there may be few other options. However, there should always be the aspiration that re-engagement remains a long-term goal. In the example above, however long and delicate the process Rosa went through, she now feels more connected, hopeful and content having been encouraged to understand herself better and to re-emerge in her own way. She also feels more conscious of early warning signals that she needs to take a break.

DEVELOPING SELF-AWARENESS

Paramount to providing proactive support is working with our young people on their self-awareness; helping them recognize when they are becoming dysregulated; knowing what they can do to regulate or to rest when they need to; understanding their unique differences; and expressing their views and preferences about what accommodations will benefit them.

If you are putting together a package to support the emotional wellbeing of a PDA person, you will need to approach this in such a way that leads you to create a collaboratively designed combination that is suited to their individual profile. Embedded in this there will need to be scope for their developing emotional literacy and self-awareness.

Julia Daunt writes:

> I regret not having had more opportunity to understand my diagnosis growing up...self-awareness is a key aspect of emotional wellbeing and makes such a difference to...decision-making as we grow up... I wanted to be understood in the context of my diagnosis but not defined by it. (Fidler & Daunt 2021)

THERAPY TO SUPPORT MENTAL HEALTH

Therapy may be recommended for those who are struggling with family dynamics, emotional regulation, depression, anxiety or behavioral challenges. Sometimes therapy is recommended to families, and where accessible there can be benefits in engaging with an objective, nonjudgmental, skilled professional. Sensory integration occupational therapists and speech and language therapies can also be very helpful, and can benefit overall wellbeing, but the focus of this section is on therapies that target mental health specifically.

There are many types of therapists, psychologists, clinical social workers, licensed clinical professional counselors, and licensed marriage and family therapists to name a few. There are also art, play and music therapists. It is important to point out that, in America, licensed mental health professionals, both those who diagnose and those who provide therapy, can only perform services in the state where they hold a license. As with other services, you will need to research what is available in your area.

There are also many kinds of therapies and approaches. Cognitive behavioral therapy (CBT) is usually recommended for people experiencing anxiety. It is often recommended at the end of neuropsychological evaluations that diagnose autism and PDA. CBT is based on the belief that individuals can have unhelpful ways of thinking and that this thinking drives problematic behaviors. DBT (dialectic behavioral therapy) is also sometimes recommended. It has a group therapy component and generally requires daily self-reporting, both of which are demands for PDAers. DBT is based on CBT and is most often recommended for people who experience intense emotions.

This style of therapy is based on the individual being able to reflect on their core beliefs, on them being self-aware enough to notice patterned responses and alter them, on being able to predict outcomes, on them being able to create imaginary scenarios and being able to flexibly problem-solve. There may therefore be significant obstacles in accessing it for individuals for whom these skills present obstacles.

Acceptance and commitment therapy (ACT) has been gaining popularity over the last few years. It is another intervention that aspires to encourage psychological flexibility to alter previous patterns of behavior. Through metaphor, paradox and experiential exercises clients learn how to reframe and amend their previous responses to certain situations. Similar challenges for PDAers as with other talking therapies, in terms of ways of thinking, apply.

Traditional therapies can have limitations for some PDA individuals. Dr. Judy Eaton, a specialist psychologist in autism in the UK, discusses the limits of some therapies. She notes that since the fundamental principle of CBT focuses on modifying or challenging automatic negative thoughts, this can be problematic to individuals who struggle with cognitive flexibility. She also points out that "since many individuals with autism have poor emotional literacy and a reduced ability to verbalize thoughts and feelings, standard CBT programs can prove problematic" (Eaton 2018).

Dr. Eaton also highlights a study by McGillivray and Evert (2014) that documents the amount of time that it can take people on the autism spectrum to establish a meaningful therapeutic relationship. The length required can be a barrier to continuing therapy, from a cost and frustration perspective. The frustration can be on the part of the client as well as the parents and therapist. The therapist may feel that continuing is unethical due to mounting costs when more time is needed.

Some individuals may have co-occurring conditions affecting their mental health, such as anxiety disorders or eating disorders. However, it is crucial that any interventions take account of the autism profile of the person so that assumptions are not made erroneously. For example, an eating disorder in an autistic person may be closely related to their sensory differences and rigid thinking, and in females may even include an aversion to menstruating, thereby creating a motivation to remain underweight.

The most important variable is not the type of therapist or the kind of therapy but is the relationship between the therapist and client. It is the relationship between the therapist and the client that makes the difference in all therapy. There is consistent evidence that the quality of the therapeutic alliance is linked to the success of psychotherapeutic treatment across a broad spectrum of types of patients, treatment modalities used, presenting problems, contexts and measurements (Stubbe 2018). With PDAers this cannot be stressed enough.

Key indicators for success from a PDA perspective overlap with the characteristics of supporting adults in all contexts, and include working with a therapist who:

- builds a trusting relationship
- is collaborative and genuine
- does not prioritize compliance
- supports and teaches self-advocacy
- proceeds at the client's pace
- does not use rewards and consequences
- is not trying to change the client's personality
- respects neurodiversity
- has a nonjudgmental attitude
- sets the agenda of each session with the client
- is playful and creative
- interacts with their client with honesty and dependability
- is prepared to do activities along with the client and to be flexible
- makes their client feel safe
- shows interest in the client's interests
- is a reflective practitioner.

Modalities for most therapies include individual, couple, family or group treatment. The aim is not to change the intrinsic nature of the person, but to target depression, anxiety, eating disorders and other issues that may be connected to or made worse by their neurodivergence. Also, the benefits and limitations of any therapy are important to understand in advance. It should not be assumed that any therapy named in this book is specifically recommended. They are listed as a resource for you to become familiar with if you are seeking interventions. It might not be the case that a type of therapy is ideally suited to a PDAer in its intended format. It is likely that it will need adapting for the various reasons set out, and in that regard, it may be helpful to seek a therapist who is prepared to be more "eclectic" in their use of approaches.

The purpose of engaging with the therapeutic process is for the individual to gain understanding of their own strengths and needs and acquire an ability to articulate these to others. Self-understanding and acceptance are crucial for happiness, as is the ability to express our inner landscapes and be validated by other people who understand us.

In finding a therapist or type of therapy that may be helpful, parents can also look at a range of options outside traditional talk therapy if they don't think that is the best choice for their child. Success is generally not dependent on a type of methodology, years of experience or type of license held. Parents can even consider expressive therapies such as art or music therapy. Therapies that are more child led can be helpful, as well as ones that are animal assisted. As with everything, it all depends on the individual. There is no one size fits all, in any of this. Since few therapists in America are trained in PDA at the time this book is being written, some families have had success in finding therapists who are trained in collaborative and proactive solutions (www.cpsconnection.com). This method, developed by Dr. Ross Greene, holds the view that "children do well if they can," and, as has been described in Chapter 4, focuses on which lagging skills and unsolved problems are causing issues. As is evident from its name, it is highly collaborative.

Sally Cat, who received a PDA diagnosis as an adult, has found a combination of therapeutic input helpful: "I've succeeded in reducing the amount of anxiety I feel through years of counselling...one-on-one Compassion Focused Therapy and a small group mindfulness course." She adds, "It's hard to quantify how much anxiety I feel because I've never been without anxiety" (Cat 2018). Indeed, it is interesting that several adults interviewed for this book mention that they did not know they had anxiety as it had always been their reality. They couldn't imagine not feeling anxious and did not know that others didn't feel this way.

Many people have found meditation and yoga effective, as well as other more easily accessible activities such as exercise, being outdoors and spending time around animals. Activities that are beneficial do not always have to include expensive specialist input.

Therapy can only work if the person is open to becoming part of the process. It is not unusual for some children with a PDA profile to struggle to attend appointments, which might be for a variety of reasons. It might be hard to handle the demands of getting dressed/ leaving the house/traveling/entering the clinic, and so on, on top of the expectations of engaging in a session with someone they might not yet know well or trust and who may be making new requests of them.

A parent reported:

> Every time I told my son that it was time to go to therapy, he had a meltdown. I had to beg and plead and practically drag him to the car. The therapist reported that she tried to get him to open up but he sat with his arms crossed against his chest and his mouth closed. I kept bringing him because I wanted to be viewed as a good parent by his doctor and the school, but now I think of it as a waste of time, energy and money. It was not the right time or the right fit.

Although this experience may not be uncommon, it is a shame that more accommodations were not explored. For instance, could it have been beneficial to look again at the time of day of the sessions and whether there was a preferable slot? What if her son had gone to sessions in his pajamas or loungewear so he avoided demands to get dressed? What did he do prior to and after sessions—could doing regulating activities at these times have helped? What if he had been able to take soothing activities to do during the session? What if the therapist had carried out the initial sessions in the car park? Could he have been allowed to enter via a quieter back door? How were the sessions and the "need" for therapy explained to him? What did *he* think was the point of the sessions? Could any special interests have been incorporated into the getting to know you phase of the therapeutic relationship? How often were demands and direct questions, however well meaning, being put to him during the session?

It is important that therapists go at a pace that builds confidence and encourages participation, which will undoubtedly mean working in a different way than they are used to with some other clients. It is critical that therapists don't give up on the sessions simply because the child is finding it hard to attend without exploring the barriers.

Part of building a trusting relationship is the ability to be there for the client when they are needed. Many of the concerns of PDA individuals feel urgent, because they are less likely to be able to manage their emotions, to tolerate waiting, to moderate their impulses and to reflect on the needs of others. Although it is understood that no therapist can be always available, and therapists need to practice self-care, telling a client who feels that they are in crisis to wait until a scheduled appointment is not straightforward. Clients need to understand that although the therapist is "there for them" they may, understandably, not be immediately available to them. This highlights the importance of having a network of people who can share the support needed so the child, and their family, are not left feeling adrift. Being in a therapeutic relationship with a PDA child, and having the degree of flexibility required, is not the right fit for every therapist. Matching a client to an appropriate therapist is, in itself, an important decision. Not having expertise in PDA does not mean that a therapist won't be able to work well with clients who fit the profile; a good match is about personal qualities plus attitudes and ethos (as is detailed in Chapter 4). In many cases, the therapist and client exploring PDA together can be very useful.

Therapists who use a trauma-informed approach are often a good fit for working with PDA individuals, because those who have a background in trauma understand the nervous system's responses of fight, flight and freeze. These stress responses are also experienced by PDAers when they are faced with demands. It should be noted that having autism and a PDA profile does not rule out trauma as a co-existing condition. Some autistic individuals feel that living in a world that is confusing and not designed to meet their needs is indeed traumatizing. Many children have had traumatic experiences in school, especially where they have experienced restraint and seclusion. The US Department of Education/Office of Civil Rights reports that 80 percent of students who were physically restrained in schools had IEPs, as had 77 percent of students who experienced seclusion (Civil Rights Data Collection 2023).

Therapists with a trauma-informed background understand the importance of making the client feel safe in their office and in building trust. Trauma-informed therapists are also collaborative and offer their clients a great deal of control in session.

Trauma relates to PDA in various ways. Psychologist Dr. Stephen Porges used the term "neuroception" to explain the brain and body's ongoing subconscious surveillance of safety and threat in the environment. His polyvagal theory suggests that the neural system constantly scans the body, via the vagus (a cranial nerve connecting the brainstem with the visceral organs), to signal when it detects a risk. If a risk is detected, that can trigger a defensive response such as flight, fright or freeze, and it will impact other responses, such as changes in heart rate, breathing and digestion. He says, "Neuroception evaluates risk in the environment without awareness. Perception implies awareness and conscious detection. Neuroception is not a cognitive process; it is a neural process without dependency on awareness." Put simply, he continues, "If our nervous system detects safety, then it's no longer defensive. When it's no longer defensive, then the circuits of the autonomic nervous system support health, growth and restoration" (Porges 2017).

Those with overly sensitive nervous systems, like PDAers, are more likely to have a trauma reaction to environments which others may view as neutral or less alarming. We can help "quieten" the neuroceptive responses by doing all we can to make them feel safe. That might include adapting their sensory environment, supporting positive interaction with safe individuals and providing a greater sense of control or of options.

Kristy Forbes (an adult PDAer and an educator and family support specialist based in Australia, who is mom to four neurodivergent children) talks about how she overprocesses her environment, sensations and emotions as "threats." She describes herself as "pathologically demand avoidant," meaning to convey by this that the way in which she is demand avoidant is an integral part of who she is.

Raelene Dundon, an educational and developmental psychologist also working in Australia, talks about trauma-informed approaches being helpful for PDAers. She writes that although she is by no means suggesting that trauma causes PDA:

> the hypervigilance to threat and high levels of anxiety experienced by individuals with PDA are similar to that demonstrated by those who have experienced trauma. The automatic reaction that an individual with PDA has to a demand is a stress response...similar to the response seen in children who have experienced trauma. (Dundon 2021)

It should not be inferred that all therapists working with PDAers need to be skilled neuroscientists. They just need to understand that anxiety is a neurological response, and it is important not to trigger that response to ensure that the client feels safe in therapy sessions.

It is sometimes helpful for parents to directly discuss with therapists what they are seeking in terms of progress or meeting specific goals. And it is important for therapists to discuss directly with parents their approaches and the process of therapy. The style and aim of therapy is to support and enhance understanding, not to "make a child behave differently." It is not about changing someone who is neurodivergent into someone who is not. It is about building acceptance and growth that will help them achieve their personal goals. This might include developing social relationships and self-awareness, managing emotions, improving independence, extending problem-solving skills or reducing anxiety. Having an open and honest discussion about the aims, approaches and markers for success will be helpful to everyone involved. It is also helpful to discuss how much privacy versus how much collaboration the child, teen or young adult welcomes.

Although family therapy may have been recommended for families who are under pressure, it is not always easy to facilitate successful family sessions. Often, a young person feels uncomfortable in a room of adults and can easily feel "ganged up on." This can cause them to either express anger or shut down. If family therapy is attempted, the therapist can take the role of interpreter for and to the young person. This can be successful in terms of explaining the messages parents are trying to communicate and, in turn, communicating to the parents on behalf of the young person how they feel and what they need.

It is crucial to understand that even if a child, adolescent or young adult attends therapy, this will not be sufficient to support them if the other environments in their life do not adapt and change to meet their needs. One hour per week of therapy cannot undo the lack of other adults co-regulating and being in settings where the pressure is too much for their nervous systems.

THERAPY FOR PARENTS AND SIBLINGS

Some parents report having negative experiences with professionals in the past and may be reluctant to seek support because of this. They report being given unhelpful advice to be stricter with their children and set firmer boundaries. Many have tried the suggestions given in an effort to be cooperative and have found that the suggestions did not work or made home life worse. Parents have noted that they felt misunderstood and judged by those who they have gone to for support.

Having followed advice to "tighten up" on boundaries, one mom said:

> Instinctively I didn't feel it was good advice, but I was worried about being judged as failing my child by not trying hard enough, so I did what they suggested. It was pretty distressing for all of us. Our daughter simply couldn't cope with even more demands, and we struggled to keep any semblance of peaceful family life while we dealt with the fallout from her anxiety and avoidance.

Hopefully, as more awareness of PDA increases, finding professionals who can provide support and assistance will become easier. Services from a therapist who understands PDA can be helpful for parents, so they have a partner in parenting their PDA child. Having a nonjudgmental, objective professional who can support their efforts can reduce stress. Helpful support can encourage parents to understand their own emotional responses when they and their child may have both become dysregulated. It is supportive to have a safe space where parents can reflect on difficult situations they have encountered, not only to understand better what might have been going on, but also to endeavor to try a different response another time. Having a therapist who reminds parents to find joy and balance in their lives as individuals is also critical. Parents frequently prioritize their child's wellbeing over their own and in the middle of a busy and unpredictable family life may not take the time to take care of themselves. Therapy sessions provide a designated time of the week to dedicate to themselves. These can be about personal issues that are impacting parenting or parenting issues. Both are valuable.

Therapeutic support to siblings can be helpful. Having a brother or sister with a PDA profile can be complex and is likely to make home life very different from some of their friends. Researchers such as Petalas et al. (2009) found higher levels of emotional issues for siblings of autistic children. Other research found increased "internalizing behaviors" (Fisman et al. 2000). It is commonly reported that siblings feel pressure to be compliant and calm and to achieve, that they can feel resentment for frequently having to accommodate the preferences of their sibling over their own, that they may be distressed seeing their parents or their sibling upset, or that they feel the weight of responsibility for their sibling as they mature.

Families need to find a dynamic of home life that works for everyone in their household. Every family is different so there is no "magic formula," but the needs of each individual are equally important so that everyone is taken care of. Living with someone who has a combination of easily activated sensitivities can be complicated and can create many reactions in others in the family. Sometimes, simply being able to express that it is tiring and distressing is helpful. And it is not always tough—PDAers have amazing qualities too. Space should always be made to notice and celebrate the joys their differences bring.

CHAPTER 6

NAVIGATING SCHOOL SYSTEMS

Whether diagnosed or not, there are children with a PDA profile who attend our schools and receive services. Information is lacking regarding how many PDA students there are in America, where they access their education, and how well their needs are recognized or met. We can get clues from what happens in the UK.

In March 2018, the PDA Society (UK) conducted an online survey in the UK called "Being Misunderstood" in which 1445 participants answered questions about the educational experiences of children and their families (Russell 2018). The results of this survey showed that:

- 70 percent of 969 young people could not tolerate their school environment or were home educated
- 71 percent of 79 adults and 70 percent of 1194 parents reported that they had found a lack of acceptance or understanding of PDA a barrier to getting relevant support.

The report highlighted that 66 percent of parents felt what their child needed was either "not considered, not properly understood, or not properly implemented." Some went on to express that where their child's autism was recognized and strategies implemented, these were directive and highly structured and had not been helpful.

Even more notable is that, sometimes, the schools did not realize that the student had been struggling until they were no longer able to attend. Many PDAers mask at school and express their anxiety in the comfort and safety of home. These students may exhaust themselves trying to fit in at school, and it can be hard for professionals to appreciate the difference between the person at home and the one they see at school.

Alice Running, mother to two PDA children, writes:

> Although school life was always a struggle for my children, they persisted with attending until it all became too much... Holding it together at school [could] only last for so long. It [was] simply too exhausting to continue pretending that everything is okay when, in fact, nearly every part of the school day is tortuous. (Running 2022)

A recent UK study into school attendance for neurodivergent children and young people (CYP) proposes "that attendance problems underpinned by emotional distress are best described as 'School Distress' (SD), given that emotional distress associated with school attendance is the core driving feature." They go on to note that "Autistic CYP displayed School Distress at a significantly earlier age, and it was significantly more enduring [plus]...demand avoidant autistic children may be especially vulnerable to School Distress" (Connolly, Constable & Mullally 2023).

Furthermore, when students find it hard to attend school regularly, their assignments and workload can pile up, causing them to be overwhelmed at the thought of returning to school. As the demands increase, the emotional tension regarding returning builds, and the likelihood of school success decreases.

A 15-year-old PDA person said:

> Some days I can go straight to school, but other days I wake up, and it's just not happening. I'm not sure why some days are different

than others, but the more it doesn't happen, the harder it gets because then I'm thinking, "I've missed four days of school. Now I really should go in today." That makes it feel like a big deal, and just ramps up the stress more.

Parents are often under pressure to make their children return to school and may have concerns about how their child's non-attendance is interpreted. Schools that put pressure on parents and hold them entirely accountable for their child's attendance often can cause those parents to act against their instincts and try to force their child to attend school. Forcing children to go to school without making further accommodations when they are already struggling invariably backfires and can make them less likely to manage school in the long term. Parents should proactively seek information concerning attendance requirements so they do not find themselves facing truancy or neglect allegations.

This book aims to prevent these difficulties from occurring because we believe that it is possible, with the proper adaptations, for schools to partner with students and families and meet the needs of their PDA children, adolescents and young adults.

There is a complicated education system in America because there are federal and state education laws. State laws differ significantly. Individual school districts also have their own procedures. Congress and the US Department of Education set federal laws and regulations. It is essential to understand what the law is in your state, established by your own Department of Education. We have not detailed legal processes here, not only because there is considerable variation across states but also because it is important to check the most up-to-date information before making any decisions that may have legal implications. Many people utilize publications from Wright's Law for information (www.wrightslaw.com). There are also Parent Training and Information Centers, which can be an invaluable resource (www.parentcenterhub.org/find-your-center).

INDIVIDUALS WITH DISABILITIES
EDUCATION ACT (IDEA)

Special education law, under the Individuals with Disabilities Education Act (IDEA), is a law that makes free public education available to eligible children with disabilities in America.

Congress reauthorized IDEA in 2004 and most recently amended IDEA through the Every Student Succeeds Act in December 2015 (Public Law 114-95), stating:

> Disability is a natural part of the human experience and in no way diminishes the right of individuals to participate in or contribute to society. Improving educational results for children with disabilities is an essential element of our national policy of ensuring equality of opportunity, full participation, independent living, and economic self-sufficiency for individuals with disabilities.

IDEA lists categories of special education (see page 48–49 for details), each with its requirements, including Autism Spectrum Disorder, Specific Learning Disability, Emotional Disturbance and Other Health Impairment. Other Health Impairment includes certain medical conditions, Attention Deficit Hyperactivity Disorder (ADHD) and anxiety. IDEA federal funds cover up to the age of 21, but some states extend the age limit for education without federal funding. In addition to the person having one of the disabilities on the list, the disability must also adversely affect their educational performance. This second criterion, determined by the school team, can be a sticking point for families whose PDA child presents very differently at school to how they are at home. Currently, many students who fit the PDA profile do not meet the criteria for qualifying for services under the autism classification. While some schools will accept a diagnosis given by an outside psychologist or pediatrician and use that to qualify a student for services, others will not. It is often just a matter of the philosophy of those in leadership roles in the school or district. Even students with a diagnosis of autism who are struggling are sometimes determined not to be eligible for an Individualized Education Plan (IEP).

An IEP outlines the student's present levels of academic achievement and performance. It also contains measurable annual goals and includes a statement of special education, related services and supplementary aids to be provided to the student, plus a statement of the program modifications or supports for school personnel that will be provided (Learning Disabilities Association of America n.d.).

Schools are more likely to qualify a student under the category of autism if they demonstrate the more widely recognized presentation of autism. As PDAers often enjoy novelty, engage in pretend play and are sociable, this can mean their profile is missed or even misdiagnosed, which can hinder their ability to qualify for services. Some educators may even doubt that they are autistic. Even when accepting the autism diagnosis, educators may have difficulty acknowledging that the school-related problems of attendance or work completion are related to their autism. Some PDA students who have difficulty maintaining emotional regulation at school may be classified as "Emotionally Disturbed." This category includes, but is not limited to, anxiety disorder, schizophrenia, bipolar disorder, obsessive-compulsive disorder and depression. Some of these diagnoses may also be included under "Other Health Impairment." Students with a PDA profile and who have co-occurring ADHD may meet the criteria for receiving services under the category of "Other Health Impaired." It is, as it sounds, not a straightforward process, and unfortunately a lot of the official language still used is negative and deficit orientated.

IDEA also states that it is a requirement that students must be educated in the "least restrictive environment" (LRE) that fits their individual needs. A LRE requirement within IDEA necessitates that:

- students with disabilities receive their education alongside their peers without disabilities to the maximum extent appropriate

- students should not be removed from the general education classroom unless learning cannot be achieved even with the use of supplementary aids and services.

The right to be placed in a non-public (private or therapeutic) school applies only if the local school district cannot provide an appropriate program. There needs to be either an IEP agreement or due process court ruling that a private placement is appropriate before a school district is required to pay for that placement. Sometimes, schools start the process because they feel they cannot educate a student within the general education classroom, and sometimes parents seek a change in placement if they think the school is not meeting their child's needs. Even if parents are granted the option of their child attending a non-public school, the school district must then find a school that is able to meet the child's unique needs with an available spot.

IDEA gives parents rights and protections, too. These are called "procedural safeguards," which are a set of ground rules for how schools work with families. The nonprofit organization Understood (www.understood.org) provides information and support to families navigating the system. Key points of procedural safeguards are that families have a right to participate in their child's education as well as access to dispute resolution options, including filing for due process if necessary.

When parents disagree with a school system regarding whether the education their child is receiving is appropriate, they may decide to hire an advocate or attorney to challenge the school district. Parents may feel they have no choice but to go down this path if they cannot come to an agreement. However, this is costly, and the process can be lengthy and can be very stressful, so collaborative solutions are the preferable route wherever possible.

SECTION 504

- - - - - - - - - -

Section 504 of the Americans with Disabilities Act guarantees that a child with a disability has equal access to an education comparable to that provided to those without disabilities. It does not have the same benefits as an IEP; students are not guaranteed to receive specialized academic instruction, and school districts have fewer requirements for documentation. Modifications and accommodations under a 504 usually refer to improving building accessibility, classroom accommodations, changes in teaching style or in how the curriculum is presented, and how understanding is assessed. They often focus on disabilities such as epilepsy, ADHD or physical disabilities. It also pertains to psychological conditions such as depression and anxiety, which can be relevant for some with a PDA profile (although this might relate to the impact, not the core characteristics of their PDA profile). The qualification includes that the disability must substantially limit one or more major life activities and substantially limit their educational performance. Standard accommodations include preferential seating and extra time on assignments or homework, but these may not be sufficient adaptations for some students. In practice, it is more likely that students who fit the PDA profile will receive a 504 plan rather than an IEP.

It is essential to remember that diagnosis or disability is not supposed to drive the IEP or 504. It should be based on the individual needs of the student. Sometimes, a circular discussion occurs when the individual's needs are not sufficiently well recognized in the first place, such that effective adaptations are also not identified.

One of the most confusing concepts in public education is that schools are not required to deliver an outstanding or even excellent education. They are required to offer an "appropriate" education that is deemed to be reasonably calculated to enable the child to make progress. The term "free appropriate public education" means special education and related services that:

- have been provided at public expense, are under public supervision, and without charge
- meet the standards of the state education agency
- include an appropriate preschool, elementary school or secondary school education in the state involved
- are provided in a way that conforms with the individualized education program required under Section 1414(d) of IDEA.

Although, as a wider society, there may be a place for a broad category that meets the needs of most children in an adequate educational environment, equally understandably, many parents want an education for their children that is better than this. During an IEP meeting, an independent professional reported hearing a parent being told by the school administrator that he sympathized with their request, but they were asking for the "Cadillac" education for their child, and he was only required to give them a "Chevy." Not surprisingly, this situation, however it may reflect the real picture, does not present a very reassuring principle for families.

DEVELOPING GOOD PRACTICES ACROSS SCHOOLS

Both public and private schools can adopt the strategies and practices described throughout this book, which can be used school-wide. There are also resources for training and certification opportunities available in America that were developed for other groups who experience anxiety or social communication differences which may benefit PDA students. Even without adopting a school-wide approach to supporting vulnerable students, almost any classroom can meet the needs of a PDA learner. Doing so involves rejecting the notion that fair and equal are synonymous. Equality for all students is about equality of access to education; it is not about treating all students the same. Each child will need a different approach in order to have the same opportunities as others. Educators need to individualize based on a student's needs.

Joe Brummer, author and mediator, combines the principles of trauma-informed education with restorative practices and uses the concept of universal precautions, known in healthcare but adapted for schools. He explains that, in preventing infectious diseases, standard precautions are taken, such as wearing gowns and hand washing. The idea is to assume that all body fluids are contaminated with something communicable, so everyone should take precautions not to spread that contamination. Since it is unknown which students have experienced trauma and which have not, all students should be treated with the same assumption that they need to feel safe. This philosophy easily applies to PDA approaches. School staff may not know who fits the PDA profile and who does not, but they can create an atmosphere based on connection and focused on student needs. He goes on to discuss demand avoidance and explains that reactivity "comes from humans wanting to protect their freedom and personal choice" (Brummer & Thorsborne 2021). In a very PDA-inclusive way, he describes the problems with using praise and suggests expressing gratitude as a more helpful response.

The Applied Educational Neuroscience© (AEN) framework developed by Dr. Lori Desautels is also trauma-responsive and incorporates current relational and brain science (Desautels 2020). It includes four pillars: educator brain and body state; co-regulation; touchpoints; and teaching students and staff about their brain and body states. The focus is not only on the students but also on the adults. Dr. Desautels focuses on relational learning and ways to organize a classroom and a school day to provide a sense of safety so students can learn. It covers brain-aligned strategies and supports which can be integrated into any classroom and benefit all students. In fact, teaching children about how their brains respond is part of the practice.

Psychologist Marshall Rosenberg developed work around non-violent communication, which has the goal of creating empathy and partnership. He refers to the differences between "power over, power with, and power within." In relational social interaction, "power over" is the use of strategies such as force, coercion and punishment/reward. "Power with" is the use of strategies like collaboration, choice/agency and personal boundaries. "Power within" is the sense of empowerment we feel when we see the way that we can impact our own experience. Power within is more likely to be born out of a "power with" dynamic than one that is "power over" (Rosenberg 1999).

Zach Morris, an educator and consultant whose work is influenced by Rosenberg, shared his philosophy of educating PDA students at the fourth annual PDA North America conference in March 2023. He described his goal for education as "to help individuals cultivate power within so that they can develop the skills to be functioning and contributing members of the community." He notes that stretching students can be an important part of education but suggests that the person teaching should ask themselves how they can provide the student with "safety inside of being challenged." Educators should understand that an individual student's experience is unique to them, and it is their job to understand what that experience is, and what their associated needs are. Facilitating learning for one child is not a simple formula that can be replicated with all learners.

Taking these models and applying them to a school-wide ethos, there can be a growing appreciation of approaches that are person-centered, prioritize emotional wellbeing, take account of sensory sensitivities, and facilitate learning through personal interests. Schools that can change their culture and embed key principles into their practices will support all students to thrive.

HOMESCHOOLING AND UNSCHOOLING

Since many students struggle with various demands at school, including attendance, many PDAers are homeschooled. It should be noted that this has not necessarily come about because parents prefer a certain education style; rather it is often the choice they have made after their child's needs were not met and/or their child was unable to attend school. Homeschooling is legal in all 50 states, but each state and each district has its own requirements for parents who homeschool their children. Parents need to know precisely what form of notification, if any, is required, as well as what type of proof of attendance is necessary. There are many differences in the documentation required according to state regarding the demonstration of learning or progress. Some require information about the parent's qualifications, curriculum used, test scores, proof of progress, and other documentation. There are even differences in the ages of compulsory attendance. The Home School Legal Defense Association (https://hslda.org) is a useful resource for checking requirements in your state.

Sometimes homeschooling begins when children have had a difficult time at school and need space to recover from the overload or from the emotional effects. There are some PDAers who experience trauma during their time at school, which may be a result of a combination of factors, including bullying or exhaustion due to masking. Homeschooling can have several benefits for young people who don't have access to an appropriate education setting. However, there are other issues that can arise. Homeschooling places a high responsibility on the family to deliver consistent supervision and a balanced curriculum. Even if there are home tutors delivering some of the teaching, families often have a large workload in coordinating and facilitating sessions, which may mean one parent is unable to work, impacting family finances. Homeschooling one child can also have an impact on siblings and parents can struggle to balance the needs of all the children in a family. There is variation in homeschool groups in different areas, so it is not always easy to link with social opportunities for the children or their parents. In some situations where a child is struggling emotionally and finds it too overwhelming to leave the house, it can be difficult for the family to go out together or to have friends visit the house, making it hard for families to get a break. For these reasons, it is wise to carefully consider the best setting for a child over time. In the same way that a school placement should be regularly reviewed to look at how well it meets the child's current needs, parents and children should have the same open, nonjudgmental conversations about homeschooling. For some families homeschooling can be an ideal long-term plan. For others, a period of homeschooling may be exactly what a child needs for a time, but particularly as children mature, they may benefit from the opportunities that education facilities can offer, if available, in relation to social relationships, sports, learning communities and access to specialized teaching or resources such as science labs.

"Unschooling" is a variation of homeschooling utilized by some parents of PDA students. Unschooling prioritizes the students' interests in their learning rather than following a set curriculum. The principle is that learning is a natural instinct and that children learn well when they are able to pursue their curiosity and to focus on what interests them in a way and at a pace that suits them. John Holt, a pioneer of unschooling, writes that:

> the idea of special learning places where nothing but learning happens no longer seems to me to make sense at all. The proper place and best place for children to learn whatever they need or want to know is the place where until very recently, almost all children learned it – in the world itself, in the mainstream of adult life. (Holt 1964)

As with homeschooling, parents need to find out the registration requirements in their area.

With both homeschooling and unschooling, there is generally an understanding that the education will be more experiential and individualized. For example, planting a vegetable garden could be a science, health education, cooking and math activity.

To demonstrate learning, the child could create a poster of the nutrients in the vegetables, or they could give a presentation on the amounts of water and sunlight for each plant to siblings or to other children in a homeschooling group. Documenting the measurements for a recipe may be a helpful learning activity, or cooking and even selling some products could be an example of an enterprise project for an older student. Activities need to evolve in line with the student's interest and engagement, but the facilitator should nonetheless be aware of what their students are learning and where their curiosity could be further extended.

Local homeschool groups can be excellent resources for advice and sharing resources. Homeschool co-ops can offer core and enrichment classes. Many areas now have a homeschool organization or association and may have access to online charter schools. For those considering homeschooling it will be beneficial to find a local group for social contact and group learning, find a methodology/learning style that suits your child, check that what you are doing meets legal requirements and consider how to log your child's progress and development.

SCHOOL-BASED BEHAVIOR INTERVENTION PLANS FOR STUDENTS WITH PDA

In their book *Better IEPS: How to Develop Legally Correct and Educationally Useful Programs*, Bateman and Linden (2006) explain that functional behavior assessments (FBA) and behavior intervention plans (BIP) are required by IDEA when a student's behavior is getting in the way of their own learning or that of others. IDEA states, "IEP teams must consider the use of positive behavioral interventions and supports and other strategies to address behavior that impedes a student's learning or that of others" (20 USC 14141(d)(3)(B)(i)).

If a student has been suspended for more than ten days, IDEA requires a "manifestation determination" to see if the behavior was a manifestation of the student's disability. If the behavior is considered to be related to the disability or the IEP was not followed, a functional behavior assessment and behavior intervention plan may be required as part of the follow-up. Although behavior plans are required, little guidance is given on what they should look like. Much of the information about what they should contain comes from litigation (Osborne & Russo 2021).

The FBA is designed to determine the function of the student's behavior and the circumstances in which it occurs. The BIP focuses on how the behavior will be addressed. The function of the student's behavior is often described simplistically, such as to gain peer attention or avoid non-preferred tasks. For students who fit the PDA profile, the behavior is generally a nervous-system response of fight, flight or freeze caused by perceived threat and anxiety. The demands of a situation are more than they can handle at that time. It can take some discussion to provide a function that is both accurate and acceptable to the school.

The American education system is one that continues to operate under a traditional behavioral approach. As explained above, this is even written into federal law. Compliance is highly valued. Those who wish to support PDA students in public and private schools will therefore have to be creative in working within the system.

Often, decisions about the degree of needs of a student are based on the behavior they display. It should be remembered, however, that behavior is a response to a stimulus. Behaviors include laughing, sharing and being affectionate as much as shouting, hitting and running away. If we understand behaviors as a form of communication, we make it our job to work out what the person is trying to communicate and why they are using this means of expressing themselves at this time. In addition, PDAers who respond differently at school than at home can sometimes perplex the adults who support them. When professionals or parents talk about "challenging behavior," what they are invariably referring to is behavior that is unhelpful, unhealthy, distressed, dysregulated or unsafe. These sorts of behaviors may challenge the adults and the situation as well as the person themselves, but they are usually an expression of distress. As educator Clare Truman reminds us, "when we discuss how to prevent distressed behavior...we should really be talking about how to reduce and manage anxiety" (Truman 2021).

Behavior is most effectively changed by proactive strategies that prevent the target behavior from occurring rather than reactive interventions that punish after the behavior occurs. The focus should be on environmental modifications, teaching strategies, supports and the instruction of new skills. A good plan looks at:

- understanding what is going on underneath the behavior
- aiming to bring about changes because they are in the child's best interests, not in an attempt to make them the same as other children who do not have a PDA profile
- supporting learning about recognizing emotions, sensations and reading the signals that indicate they are becoming dysregulated or are in a situation where they are at risk of becoming overwhelmed
- teaching effective and positive ways to express distress or displeasure
- not repeatedly putting the student in situations that are likely to be overloading for them.

Any strategies, supports and teaching styles that may help the student should be included in the plan and should be as specific as possible. Ideally, the student should also be included in planning so the whole process is collaborative.

For a student with a PDA profile the process of exploration should take the following into account:

- Consideration of the reason for the behavior; for example, maybe the student is anxious about doing a task that they don't feel confident in completing successfully; they may be confused about a social element of a task that requires group work; the task may not appeal to their interests and they may struggle to understand its purpose; they might be sensitive to the level of demand in the task itself or by the direct way it was presented to them; they may be impulsive and experience sudden mood swings.

- Thinking about whether the student may benefit from an indirect way of presenting the task; may need to have some element of control and choice within the task or to delegate certain aspects of the task; may find it easier to complete if it can be reframed around their strengths or can be postponed or completed outside the lesson or classroom; may benefit from regulating activities before, during and/or afterwards.
- Considering how we can help the student explain why they feel unable to complete the task just now; how they can develop problem-solving that encourages other ways to achieve a positive outcome; whether they can go to an agreed safe place and talk to an identified safe person if they feel they need to leave class; how they can access activities known to regulate them, then return to the task or classroom.
- Taking care that the student is not repeatedly put in situations where they receive too many anxiety-provoking direct demands, or where their sensory sensitivities are regularly overloaded. A personal profile (such as the example in Chapter 7) needs to be developed to identify sensitivities, along with the student's awareness of their needs and an accessible menu of regulating strategies.

The school team will select target behaviors to focus on. Frequently the list is long and vague. Unfortunately, the selection sometimes includes behaviors that are helpful for the student, such as being out of their seat. It is more effective to focus on one or two carefully selected target behaviors that are well defined. Behaviors such as non-compliance, being disrespectful or not listening are poor options for target behaviors. As with the target behaviors, each support or strategy must be included separately. When writing a behavior plan, it will also be helpful to refer to the approaches outlined in Chapter 4.

As PDA children and teens don't respond well to rewards and consequences, this can prove challenging in developing a plan because, generally, behavior plans focus on these strategies. Schools may be very proud of their positive reinforcement options and it can be confusing to some staff that even rewards can be problematic for some students.

Once supports and strategies are in place, they need to be reviewed regularly. Baseline data should be taken before interventions begin, with data taken on a regular basis to test if the interventions are working to reduce target behaviors.

The behavior plan also covers what happens when there are challenges and crisis situations. Schools generally tend to write in the use of whichever crisis management program they are trained in, which often includes physical restraint. Although, of course, there is a duty of care in education settings to keep everyone safe, the use of physical restraint is intended to be considered only as a last resort, to be used once all other proactive strategies have been exhausted and there is imminent danger. Making this decision can be complex. In addition, when the nervous systems in supporting adults are heightened, they may make decisions about the use of physical intervention that don't always align with how they would ordinarily respond. Physical restraint can lead to physical and/ or emotional harm as well as damaging the relationship with the student and their family. Moreover, once physical restraint starts to be used, there is a risk of it becoming more common practice, which in turn reduces the prioritization of proactive approaches. The use of time-out/seclusion is also problematic and can occur much too frequently. The Alliance Against Seclusion and Restraint is a helpful resource in this area (https://endseclusion.org).

Some schools include suspension and expulsions in the behavior plan. These are unhelpful for students who struggle and who need to be able to build a trusting relationship with the school. Sometimes, plans will refer to blanket statements following the school discipline policy which, although providing context, will need adaptation for individual students. Parents should be prepared for these discussions and be supported through them as they can be complicated.

The process of creating a school-based behavior plan should first focus on the student's personality and characteristics. There should be lots of discussion between members of the IEP team, including families as well as relevant professionals, regarding which behavior to focus on and why, along with understanding the underlying reasons for the behavior. Discussion should inform the interventions and should reflect the student's views where possible. The main purpose of a behavior plan is to meet the individual's needs. It is not about forcing a child to fit into an existing system that is the wrong shape for them.

CHAPTER 7

CREATING A FRAMEWORK FOR SUPPORT

Having explored many themes that have an impact on families and professionals, we want to provide some tools to help with planning next steps and creating a framework for support. All recommendations made throughout this book are suggested on the basis that they are personalized for the individual, so when you are planning and coordinating provision it is paramount that the unique person you support is kept at the center of all your discussions. We have tried to set out some common themes and principles that may be helpful.

Writing a framework is equally relevant to individuals who attend school or college and those who don't. It can be used by families as well as by professionals who work in a range of services. A framework for support should put high value on learning, but to be clear, that does not only refer to learning that happens in places like schools or that is delivered by teachers. Children, teenagers and young adults do not have to go to school to learn; learning happens throughout our lives, and when we are young there is much to discover. Learning is not only about academic subjects but also about understanding ourselves, other people, real-life situations and dilemmas, solving problems and becoming autonomous.

Sometimes supporting adults find themselves focusing on how to facilitate independence. However, being independent is not about doing everything on your own. It is more beneficial to view independence as autonomy. Autonomy is about having the ability and the freedom to make decisions that suit you as an individual. That doesn't mean individuals shouldn't take advice or can't delegate aspects of implementing a decision to others; it is about them knowing what they want, understanding why it will work for them and being empowered to make decisions accordingly. In this regard there is also an important element of interdependence.

WRITING A PERSONAL PROFILE

PDAers will have their needs better understood and met when key themes that are unique to them are acknowledged. Doing that starts with creating an individual profile that notes their preferences, their important people, animals and activities in their life, what we already know tends to upset or to soothe them, what they are currently interested in and who is involved in collaborating to meet their education, health and social care needs.

As part of our consultation work, it has been helpful to use the personal profile as a starting point to gather this information. It is important that all those involved have a way to contribute to this part of the process, including the family and the person themselves where that is achievable. If the individual is not able to contribute directly, there should be space created for those who know them well to represent their views.

Of course, any information is only as useful as how well it was gathered and how well it is utilized, so we must also consider whether the personal profile gives us enough of the right detail, and if not, from where/who and how we can endeavor to fill the gaps. That is how we can be reflective and personalized, whatever our role is in supporting individuals, so in this regard you may find you want to add to or change some of the headings in the profile tool that follows.

PERSONAL PROFILE

Name	Date of birth	Date completed	Learning setting
		Age at time of completing	Teaching input provided by
Diagnoses (if any)	Names of professionals involved	Roles of professionals involved	Those who contributed to this profile
Strengths	Likes and preferences	Hobbies and interests	Views expressed, either directly or indirectly, by the child about their aspirations, needs, choices, etc.
Activities known to regulate and soothe	Experiences known to cause stress or dysregulation	Strategies known not to be effective currently	Strategies known that are often helpful currently
Health needs	Sensory differences	Social and communication needs	Other people who support
Individual's views of their priorities	Learning priorities	Emotional wellbeing priorities	Family priorities

IDENTIFYING PRIORITIES

Based on the information you will have gathered from completing the personal profile, you should now have built a collaborative picture and you will have identified the most relevant people to contribute to identifying high, medium and lower priorities. Using priority rating charts, as detailed in Chapter 4, is an effective way to inform planning the next steps.

Although there is space in the priority rating chart for an agreed review date, that shouldn't limit more frequent reflection and updates should circumstances require.

TRACKING OUTCOMES

Teachers, parents and therapists will want to know the impact of their support. It is important that what we do with an individual should be led by what we have decided are the agreed priorities, and that we hold onto these broad themes as we guide them in their development. Some days or situations are trickier than others, so it is going to be helpful if we have a flexible approach to setting, assessing and reviewing outcomes. Ultimately, children will be adults a lot longer than they are children, so we should keep a long-term view on promoting good adult outcomes. Although it may seem quite a way off for young children, some long-term goals are actually very well aligned with what we might be encouraging anyway. For instance, thinking about preparation for employment does not have to have a focus on qualifications and interview techniques. It could include being able to make informed choices; expressing a view, in particular discussing a viewpoint where there is a difference of opinion; organizing equipment for a task; developing an understanding of concepts around budgeting; navigating public transportation; and developing enough self-awareness and self-advocacy to know what adjustments to a task or environment are helpful.

When it comes to assessing progress that has been made in learning, there are a number of questions it can be useful to ask. Supporting adults may have different perspectives. They will have their own roles and relationships with the individual which will carry both strengths and weaknesses. That means supporting adults may perceive different aspects of an individual's profile as well as their learning, maybe even between one parent and the other, which is why it is important to coordinate and integrate those perceptions.

Reflective questions regarding progress tracking include those shown in the chart that follows.

PROGRESS TRACKING REFLECTION PROMPTS	
Why did we set that as a learning target? What were we hoping to achieve? How did we generate the learning target?	
What constitutes evidence of progress toward learning targets?	
How are we recording evidence? How are we cross-referencing evidence with the learning targets? How are we capturing progress made across settings?	
Who has overview of the progress made? How often is it logged and reviewed?	
At what stage do we set new learning targets? For example, at the start of a new year? Depending on progress made on previously set targets?	
How are we deciding how much progress has been made? What are the categories we will use to measure progress? How are they defined?	
How is progress integrated into other data systems used by our family or our organization?	
How well do the outcomes align with requirements of services or entities involved?	

Completing this proforma should include contributions from all those supporting the PDAer, ideally incorporates the student's perspectives, and can be linked to collaborative discussions about priority setting or planning. It will be helpful to refer back to Chapter 4 as you explore these points.

When you are assessing progress it is also important to have an agreed process to determine what progress looks like. You will need to combine what you record and how you record it and use this data to inform where you feel learning is up to.

What is recorded should be relevant to learning intentions set and should reflect priorities. Although it is tempting to come up with quantitative data that can generate clearly charted progress, this will not capture all the significant information, much of which needs recording as qualitative data in a narrative form. Collaborative working will enable you to use information from parental record-keeping, professionals' feedback and even the individual's own log to develop ways of translating qualitative data into quantitative, whether you use summative or formative assessments. You may use categories such as the following:

- **NYD**, Not yet developed—not confident in this area, not aware of most aspects of this learning or of the benefits of developing this skill.
- **ED**, Early development—some first steps in working toward an early understanding but unreliable. Needs considerable guidance to carry out tasks in this area.
- **WD**, Well developed—signs of understanding and starting to be more reliably demonstrated, but still needs some prompting.
- **E**, Established—good understanding and often implemented independently and spontaneously without adverse response. Where this skill is not utilized it is usually because there is an understandable rationale or dysregulation. Able to identify when this skill could be useful.

- **S,** Secure—good understanding and demonstrated across settings including being able to use as part of independent problem-solving. There is awareness of own ability in this area and confidence in using it.

The following is an example of learning intentions, based on the Autism Education Trust Progression Framework (Autism Education Trust 2023), set for a 17-year-old student in the UK who has not been able to attend school regularly so has a team of home tutors, a therapist and a social care personal assistant.

★

Name . . . .

Progress tracking for academic year 2024/2025

Learning intentions (LIs) collaboratively identified on (date): . . . .

Evidence collated regarding progress toward by regular feedback from Multidisciplinary Team.

Key:

NYD, Not yet developed – not confident in this area, not aware of most aspects of this learning or of the benefits of developing this skill.

ED, Early development – some first steps in working toward an early understanding but unreliable. Needs considerable guidance to carry out tasks in this area.

WD, Well developed – signs of understanding and starting to be more reliably demonstrated, but still needs some prompting.

E, Established – good understanding and often implemented independently and spontaneously without adverse response. Where this skill is not utilized it is usually because there is an understandable rationale or due to dysregulation. Able to identify later that this skill could have been useful.

S, Secure – good understanding and demonstrated across settings including being able to use as part of independent problem-solving. There is awareness of own ability in this area and generally confident in using this skill.

Learning intentions: (age when LIs set ....)	Date LI set	Baseline when set	First quarter	Second quarter	Third quarter	Fourth quarter
Copes with proximity of others in a public space	06.23.24	WD	WD	WD	E	E
Engages in interactive exchange with adult (when in the community)	06.23.24	ED	ED	ED	ED	WD
Makes contact with organizations online, by phone or in person to plan activities	06.23.24	NYD	NYD	ED	ED	ED
Complete tasks using math and English skills based around functional situations and interests	06.23.24	ED	ED	WD	WD	E
Engages in social exchange within leisure activity with familiar and unfamiliar adults	06.23.24	ED	ED	ED	ED	WD
Plans a journey or trip out. This includes identifying a venue of interest, planning travel arrangements and budgeting the trip	06.23.24	ED	ED	ED	ED	ED
Demonstrates understanding of benefit entitlement and how much this equates to	06.23.24	NYD	NYD	NYD	ED	ED
Manages own money. This includes managing a weekly budget for travel, visits and meals out	06.23.24	ED	ED	WD	WD	WD

Skill	Date					
Prepares to make a meal with support. Plans what ingredients will be needed to make a preferred dish	06.23.24	NYD	NYD	ED	ED	ED
Prepares a meal with support. Shows awareness of food preparation, hygiene and safety	06.23.24	NYD	ED	ED	ED	ED
Identifies own emotions at complex level, including those relating to past events and future experiences	06.23.24	ED	ED	ED	WD	WD
Takes part in planning and preparing strategies to manage own emotions and behaviour	06.23.24	ED	ED	ED	ED	ED
Makes healthy choices in relation to sleep	06.23.24	WD	WD	E	E	E
Takes action to manage own sensory needs	06.23.24	ED	ED	ED	WD	WD
Understands her health needs and contributes to her health action plan with support	06.23.24	ED	ED	WD	WD	WD
Crosses road safely with minimal prompt (for reassurance only)	06.23.24	ED	WD	WD	WD	E
Pays for items in a shop or online, by card or cash	06.23.24	ED	E	WD	E	E
Recognizes own achievements	06.23.24	ED	WD	WD	WD	E

★

Analysis at the end of the year:

Total learning intentions set: 18

No of LIs in which progress made: 17

Decline: 0

Progress increased by one category: 12 or 66.6%

Progress increased by more than one category: 5 or 27.7%

Percentage of progress made of at least one category in learning intentions set: 94.4%

Contributions to summaries from:

Home tutor, therapist, social worker, parents, sibling, individual themselves

Additional comments regarding tracking progress:

Progress regarding planning a trip out was hampered by broken leg which affected confidence and required lengthy recovery period

The value of a system like this for individuals, whether they are in formal settings or at home, is that it provides a means to set relevant and personalized goals. The progress data it produces can supplement evidence within settings where an individual is following a highly personalized curriculum or can contribute to data required by a district or state where individuals are having their needs met at home.

PREPARATION FOR ADULTHOOD

An alternative approach is to work the other way around, and instead of building from childhood toward adult outcomes, you can track back from adult goals. There are some key areas that preparation for adulthood generally includes. These fall broadly under the following headings:

- **Employment:** As mentioned earlier, this is not necessarily about going straight into paid work but is about breaking down the skills that having a job, whether a paid or voluntary role, will require. Initially that may be about organizing time and resources; sustaining focus on a task until it is completed; applying for jobs; developing self-advocacy skills; giving and receiving guidance or suggestions; developing IT skills; managing time; working with others; and being able to follow procedures.
- **Good health:** Aspects of this area will include recognizing illness or pain and being able to identify or express the sensations; understanding one's own health conditions; engaging with medical appointments; understanding the purpose of prescribed medication and managing to take as required; taking care of general health needs regarding balanced diet,

sleep hygiene and regular exercise; and good mental health and emotional regulation.

- **Friends, relationships and community:** This will incorporate understanding social situations; building, maintaining and repairing social relationships; recognizing feelings and expressing them positively; having healthy romantic relationships; being assertive but not unnecessarily confrontational; accessing community amenities; finding and joining social interest groups.

- **Independent living:** This area includes problem-solving; making choices; recognizing one's own needs and profile and having the self-advocacy skills to express them; building a network of others who can support; predicting consequences; and managing everyday tasks related to taking care of personal needs and chores within living accommodation, including cleaning, shopping, budgeting and cooking.

All of these are aspects of development that can be incorporated into teaching and learning opportunities for children well before they reach adult years, and will put them in a much stronger position to thrive as they mature.

If we can help young people to become more self-reliant, and more confident in who they are, at the same time as we make progress in wider society to be more accepting and understanding of difference, we should be able to achieve more positive outcomes for everyone.

PROTECTING TIME FOR EMOTIONAL WELLBEING

We have covered issues regarding emotional wellbeing throughout this book, particularly in Chapter 5. When it comes to putting together a framework for children, adolescents and young adults, it is paramount to support their emotional wellbeing. This includes helping them to identify their feelings and to express them, work out what helps to regulate them and how they can access those things in various settings, and for them to be included in plans that build in time for recovery as required.

It may be helpful to incorporate ways to log emotional wellbeing that present opportunities for individuals to develop their understanding as well as to track progress over time. You may like to use the questionnaire shown below, or to adapt it to the individual you know. We would always suggest, as with other interventions, that it is carried out collaboratively, so it is important to cross-reference any data collected. That means any questionnaires that are completed by parents, professionals and other supporting adults are compared, while having a separate way to capture information from the individual themselves.

EMOTIONAL WELLBEING QUESTIONNAIRE FOR SUPPORTING ADULTS

Name of individual:

Completed by:

Date completed:

Relationship to individual:

To what extent are they impacted by:	Very little					all the time
	0	1	2	3	4	5
Sensory sensitivities (please give details)						
Everyday expectations, e.g. washing, going out (please give details)						
Puberty, gender identity or other issues related to maturing						
Other mental health needs (please give details)						
Physical health, e.g. other medical conditions or impact of medication, attending appointments (please give details)						

Please rate the following within your experience of the individual's profile:

	Strongly agree	Mostly agree	Neutral	Mostly disagree	Strongly disagree	Comments
It is easy to engage them in interaction with familiar people						
They know what they want and are able to make choices						
They recognize simple emotions in themselves and communicate how they are feeling, e.g. sad, happy, mad, scared						
They can identify what might have caused their emotion, e.g. excited about a new game, sad about a disappointment						
They can recognize simple emotions in other people, e.g. sad, happy, mad, scared						
They can identify what might have caused others' emotions, e.g. happy to see someone, mad that something is broken						
They are aware of their sensory needs and of what sensations cause them agitation						
They use strategies to self-regulate, including personal interests, withdrawing, self-stimulatory activities						
They can accept calming strategies from others that will help them regulate						

★

	Strongly agree	Mostly agree	Neutral	Mostly disagree	Strongly disagree	Comments
They can independently seek or request activities that they know will soothe them						
They have positive social relationships with: Key individuals at home Key individuals out of home Most people they know						
They demonstrate awareness of the impact of their responses on other people they know (positively or negatively)						
It is common to have periods of time when they seem distressed						
Their moods frequently swing from high to low						
They have specific anxieties or phobias (please give details)						
They are able to reflect on periods of dysregulation, sometime after the event, and express their perspective						
They have regular periods of time when they seem content						
They pass comment on wishing their circumstances were different						
They use any self-harming behaviors						

Additional comments would be helpful regarding:

If they have regular periods of time of being either distressed or content, what are the usual circumstances that have contributed to this?

. . . .

. . . .

. . . .

. . . .

. . . .

Do you have any specific concerns about their wellbeing?

. . . .

. . . .

. . . .

. . . .

. . . .

Are they currently accessing any activities or professional input to support their emotional wellbeing? If so, please give details.

. . . .

. . . .

. . . .

. . . .

. . . .

EMOTIONAL WELLBEING PROMPT QUESTIONS FOR CHILDREN, TEENAGERS AND YOUNG ADULTS

The following questions provide prompts to help when gathering information about the wellbeing and self-awareness of the child, adolescent or young adult you support. For reasons that hopefully will be obvious, **it is *not recommended* that you present this list of questions directly to a PDAer.** The list is intended to guide a structured conversation. It may work well to bring the questions into ordinary conversations over a period of time and you may need to amend the questions in a way that suits the individual you know. You will need to personalize the process; we are simply providing some thoughts regarding what would be valuable to explore.

- What are your hobbies or interests?
- What are you good at?
- Where do you feel most content?
- Where do you like going outside the family home?
- Do you go anywhere regularly, such as swimming, clubs?
- Do you go to school/college/home education groups?
- If so, how is that for you?
- Who do you like spending time with?
- Can you say what you like about being with them?
- Do you find it hard to do everyday things that you know *how* to do like getting dressed/going out/chores?
- Can you usually tell how you feel? Happy/sad/mad/anxious?
- If you do have these feelings, do you usually know why you feel that way?
- Can you describe what sorts of things make you feel happy/ mad/sad/anxious?
- What do you enjoy doing on your own?
- What helps you feel calm?
- Are there things you would like to do more of? To learn more about?

- Can you usually tell if you feel hungry/tired/in pain?
- Do you often feel unwell? If so, what does that feel like for you?
- What does a good day look like for you?
- What would a bad day look like for you?
- Do you have any ideas about what you would like to do in the future?
- Are there things you often worry about?
- How would you describe yourself?
- How do you think other people would describe you?
- Are there physical sensations that you usually either strongly like or dislike?
- Do you usually eat and sleep well?
- Is there anything that you feel people who know you don't understand about you?

MAKING ACCOMMODATIONS

PDAers will need some accommodations across the arenas of their lives. Some may need more in certain areas than others, so it is important not to make assumptions about what any one PDA person needs. It is also important neither to overestimate their abilities nor to underestimate them. Just because someone may benefit from additional accommodations during a period of change or of overload does not mean that accommodation will be necessary long-term. Similarly, just because an individual has seemed to be managing certain tasks, if their circumstances or wellbeing alters that may need reviewing. This point brings us back to the need for ongoing collaborative discussions, listening to the individual's own voice and reviewing input to ensure it still provides what they need.

Beneficial accommodations might include those made within learning settings that have been explored in Chapter 4 as well as others that may be more relevant to home, which have been discussed in Chapter 3. Examples of accommodations for young adults could include:

- eating a ready-made meal rather than cooking from scratch on days when the demand to cook is too great, as that is preferable to not eating
- starting work at 11 a.m. on the basis that they struggle with mornings and need additional processing time to get organized for their day
- getting a lift to and from college so that their emotional and sensory energies are not so depleted by coping with a journey on public transportation that they are unable to concentrate in class
- being able to pin their ID badge to their backpack rather than wear it around their neck to avoid sensory sensitivities.

CREATIVE COLLABORATIVE PACKAGES

Ideally there would be a simple strategy for meeting the needs of PDAers that was consistent and clear, but systems in America are complicated by the variation between localities and not all services being familiar with PDA profiles. A model of good practice could, in theory, be developed at a local level and, who knows, maybe one day even at a national level. It would have at its heart the principle of truly collaborative practice. It could look a little like the system that is used in the UK whereby some children, teenagers and young adults with additional needs have education, health and care plans (EHCPs). The principle is that a person's whole needs are taken into account. Plans should take account of needs in all areas of development, wellbeing, health and learning. Children, teenagers and young adults who are suitable for an EHCP are identified in the UK as those who have a learning difficulty or disability that means they have significantly greater difficulty than the majority of others of the same age, which prevents them from making use of the facilities generally provided in regular settings (Department for Education 2015).

The headings that feature in EHCPs to describe the areas of needs include:

- communication and interaction
- cognition and learning
- social, emotional and mental health
- physical and sensory needs.

Also included are the child's perspectives and the parents' views.

It is by no means an ideal model, and there are a number of challenges in the UK regarding waiting lists, agreeing the content of plans, and implementing them, but there are some helpful aspects of their intention and purpose which could be incorporated in developing future support systems in America.

EHCPs can apply to children, teenagers and young adults who are attending an educational placement or who are currently receiving their education "other than at school." This is not the same as elective home-education; it is whereby, for reasons related to their additional needs, they are unable to attend a suitable placement, so they may receive their education via a series of tutors, therapists and other individuals who support them. These arrangements will be regularly reviewed (at least once a year) and at some point there might be a return to a formal education setting.

A framework that would be greatly beneficial for PDAers is a model of a hub, representing the center of a wheel. It would be the role of the "hub manager" to liaise with all partners including the family. The hub manager would hold the responsibility for coordinating all partners as required, for sharing paperwork and reports, for chairing meetings and for facilitating regular reviews. There do not need to be rigid arrangements regarding who takes on this role—it could be someone from any of the services or partnerships involved. The priority is about retaining collaborative working practices and ensuring that all services are coordinating with each other.

SUPPORTING YOUNG ADULTS

It is hoped that young adults will have received enough support throughout their childhood years to be in a positive position by the time they reach young adulthood. If that is not quite the case, it is never too late to implement the approaches outlined in this book: they will just need adapting to the current situation. Some may continue to live with their families, others may have moved to live independently. What matters most is their ability to thrive and to enjoy a fulfilling life. That can be achieved in numerous ways, and is not defined by income, housing or social media image.

The examples below demonstrate different roles that individuals play in the lives of our young adults. There will be variations on these themes for all of us. Most of us living mature, independent, autonomous adult lives have a network of friends, family and professionals who support us and with whom we share chores. That doesn't necessarily mean we all have specialist people involved in our everyday life, but we certainly may rely on a best friend, an emergency plumber, a sibling, partner or neighbor. These people are members of our "hubs" or networks.

Let's start with Maria.

MARIA

Maria is 22 years old, living in her own apartment in Chicago. Her network includes:

- Bill—Maria's neighbor, who reminds her when to put out the trash and does it for her if required.

- Dr. Lopez—Maria's individual therapist, working with her to treat her depression.
- Rosa—Maria's aunt, who is supporting her to use public transportation.
- Wendy Jones—Maria's art teacher, who runs a small-group class that Maria attends. Maria is starting to make friends at the art group.
- Glen Flores—Maria's supervisor at work, who meets with her at the start and end of every shift to help her plan her working day and to talk through any issues that have arisen.
- Karen—family friend, who gives support on bill paying and apartment maintenance.
- Tony and Myrtle—Maria's parents, who have a meal with her most weekends and go grocery shopping with her once a week.

DAVID

David is 25. He lives in a shared apartment with a friend, called Jim, who he met at the Dungeons and Dragons group he attends.

- Jim—David's roommate. They have an arrangement that one of them cleans the kitchen and the other cleans the bathroom. Jim is comfortable with David choosing which chore he wants to do that week, and he picks up the other. They cook food separately and have a small fridge each. They give each other advance notice if the other wants to have a friend come over. They still go to D&D meetings together at weekends.
- Alice—David's colleague at work. They travel to work together.
- Ken—David's boss. Ken meets David on Mondays to help

him prioritize which work tasks are most time-sensitive for the week.

ALAN

Alan is 23 years old. He works full time and lives with his parents and Evie, his younger sister, who is 19.

- Sophia and Steve—Alan's parents, who help Alan with organizing his administrative tasks such as banking, medical appointments and any tasks that require filling out forms.
- Evie—Alan's sister. Like Alan, she enjoys hiking and often goes on trips with Alan. This is becoming a bit of a family tradition they both find fun.
- Hudson—Alan's friend at work. They tend not to chat much during the working day but Hudson supports Alan if there are any issues arising in the office and discusses with him how he might handle certain situations. They sometimes go for a beer after work.
- Bruno—Alan's mechanic. Alan met Bruno when he regularly fixed Alan's beloved old truck. Bruno has taught Alan some basic mechanics and they have been to Monster Truck events together.
- Carmen—Alan's maternal grandma, who lives a 20-minute drive away. Alan has always been very close to her and visits her often. Since Carmen's husband died, Alan helps her with a lot of chores such as gardening, laundry and shopping. He doesn't participate in these chores at home, so this is an important context in which he is learning these skills.

ROBYN

Robyn is 19. They identify as non-binary and live with their parents.

- Amy and Josh—Robyn's parents, who take care of the majority of household tasks such as laundry, shopping and preparing most main meals. Robyn is encouraged to prepare snacks themselves.
- Leah—Robyn's cousin. They chat online most days via a shared interest in PlayStation games.
- Phoenix—Robyn's friend, who leads the LGBTQ+ group that they attend weekly. Robyn often has a meal out with Phoenix after the meetings.
- Gloria—a choir leader where Robyn attends one evening a week. They do not always like to participate in concerts but are always welcome to do so.
- Lisa—a friend from a homeschool group they attended together. They like to go to the mall together at weekends to browse the book stores.
- Lauren—a family friend who lives nearby and is helping teach Robyn to drive.
- Andrew—a neighbor who helps the family with grocery shopping if needed and has Robyn over to watch sports so that Amy can take their younger siblings to the park or the movies when Robyn doesn't want to join them.
- Dr. Delgado—has known Robyn for ten years and has built a positive relationship. Robyn is now able to participate in medical appointments and can talk directly to Dr. Delgado about their health.

Using the diagram shown in Figure 7.1, it is possible to map an individual's network. Carrying out this process can also highlight where there may be gaps that need filling.

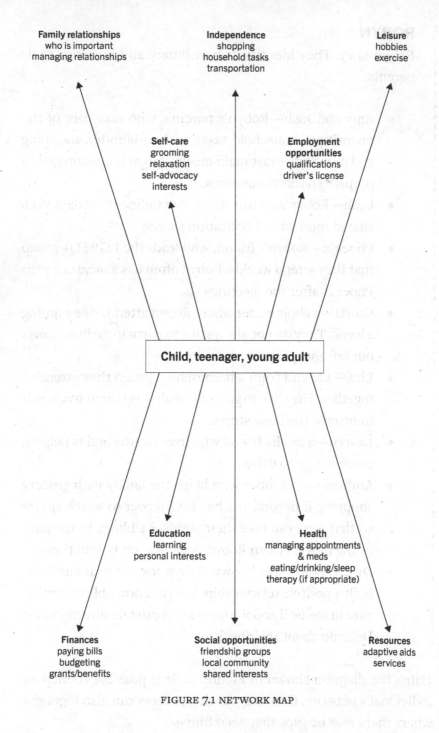

Family relationships
who is important
managing relationships

Independence
shopping
household tasks
transportation

Leisure
hobbies
exercise

Self-care
grooming
relaxation
self-advocacy
interests

**Employment
opportunities**
qualifications
driver's license

Child, teenager, young adult

Education
learning
personal interests

Health
managing appointments
& meds
eating/drinking/sleep
therapy (if appropriate)

Finances
paying bills
budgeting
grants/benefits

Social opportunities
friendship groups
local community
shared interests

Resources
adaptive aids
services

FIGURE 7.1 NETWORK MAP

MANAGING A NETWORK

Many of us are familiar with the saying that it takes a village to raise a child, meaning that it is a shared endeavor and will benefit the whole community if everyone is included. Some PDAers may have fallen through the net of support and families may not feel they have access to the support networks they have needed. Where this has happened it is regrettable, but it can be rebuilt. What we are trying to demonstrate here is a model for achieving that network. We acknowledge that it may seem highly aspirational to some of our readers, but that shouldn't stop us remaining optimistic.

It may take many years to refine and recruit the team, and available services are going to differ greatly depending on individual situations and geographical locations. Initially the role of hub manager may fall to parents, although it is hoped they would be well supported by local resources. Ideally, over time, the role will be taken on increasingly by the young person themselves. To be clear, this is not to suggest that they should be shouldering the responsibility of an unrealistic number of expectations; it is about them playing a vital role in delegating tasks and choosing who can best represent their views. It is important that the young person is not viewed as passive, compliant or uncritical in the decisions made around them and about them, but that they have an active voice that is heard and incorporated into any plans.

Maja Toudal, a Danish autistic psychologist, author and educator, writes:

> We need you to catch us, not carry us... Everyone needs to know that someone will catch them if they fall; but being there with your arms stretched out ready to catch, does not mean holding us down when we try to jump, or lifting us up so we can reach without trying. (Toudal 2022)

She has also developed what she calls an "energy accounting" system. This is a process in which an individual identifies and quantifies activities that add value to their capacity, or available "funds," and other activities that deplete or spend those funds. The idea is to remain in credit. An example is shown below.

Energy withdrawal	Energy deposit
Wearing new shoes –60	Cycling around the lake +65
Going to a store –80	Stroking the cat +60
Hot weather –25	Organizing my rock collection +70
Flying insects –50	Watching my favorite show +60
Having an appointment –85	Hanging out with Logan +50
Eating a meal with other people –40	Sleeping well +80
Bus journey –50	Time alone in my room +70
Total –390	Total +455

Days when there is a deficit in energies or events that are predicted to be "high cost" should be balanced out as soon as possible.

Of course, the same is true of the supporting adults, or other family members, on the understanding that it is hard to help anyone else when you are dysregulated yourself.

SUPPORTING THE ADULTS WHO SUPPORT THE PDA INDIVIDUALS

PDAers are wonderful individuals. They can also be complex and tiring to support. Even where there are networks of dedicated and wise people supporting them, in a variety of roles, there can still be times when those networks are stretched and supporting adults are emotionally depleted. That doesn't mean those people are not committed or well-intentioned, simply that life continues to happen to all of us and our capacity fluctuates. Therefore, it is an integral part of a positive, functioning network that consideration is given to supporting the people who support the PDA individual. As with everything else, this will also need to be personalized, but there are some key elements to build in, including space to do the following:

- **Pace everyone's energy and stamina:** Different people will bring varying degrees of energy and stamina, and there will no doubt be multiple demands on their resources as an individual. There may be times when one person, however closely they have previously been involved, may benefit from reducing their input for a period of time.

- **Liaise and reflect:** We have labored the notion of collaboration throughout the book, but to do this effectively will require a time commitment for liaison across the team, and for reflection.

- **Rotate key supporting adults:** This is more easily achieved where there is a wider network around a PDAer, which is another reason to build a viable team. It is typically hardest to put into place where a child is at home and there are not many other supporting adults in the picture. Friends, neighbors, local groups and wider family can be a resource here. Professionals should remain conscious of a family's networks and consider when, where and how frequently parents can access the support they may need too.

- **Have clarity regarding roles and responsibilities** across the network. This is needed most where there are a number of professionals involved who will have their own area of focus. It can still be beneficial to have a "hub manager" to coordinate the input of these people. Where a network is more informal it can also be helpful to gain clear messages from supporting adults about what they are able to provide and how often.

- **Communicate openly and constructively:** Collaboration is fundamental, but so is communication and kindness. It will help if there is an atmosphere whereby nonjudgmental and constructive conversations are welcomed which seek views from across the network. It might be useful to have regular catch-up meetings to facilitate this, however informally.

- **Recognize that all members of the network are individuals** with their own needs and their own character. Although it is advisable to identify core priorities and approaches, it is also important to understand that the people providing their input to the network are also individuals. They will need to have scope to develop their own relationship with the PDAer which suits their character and makes the most of their strengths. They do not all need to endeavor to try to be the same as each other. In fact, sometimes a change of personality can shift the mood and bring a new energy to an interaction.

- **Be aware of potential burnout** if untenable pressure is placed on any one person. Sometimes there is considerable load carried by a very small number of people. Where children or teenagers attend school this may be their case worker or similar. At home it is likely to be a parent, usually their mother. There are a number of online support groups that families may find helpful, and professional services might be available in some areas, but essentially it is vital to prevent anyone from reaching burnout.

The most central point of a framework that functions well and meets the needs of both the PDA individual and the people who support them is that it is sustainable. If you are involved in creating a framework, keep this in mind, so that you balance what is being offered and expected of supporting adults not only now, but moving forward.

CHAPTER 8

CONCLUDING COMMENTS

The PDA effort in America is still in its infancy. Awareness has been building but there is so much further to go. The PDA Society continues to be a source of information and support. They list resources throughout Europe along with South Africa, Australia and New Zealand. The world is paying attention, and finally, things are happening closer to home. We hope to follow the path led by the UK while learning from their journey so we can make progress quickly and broadly.

This book is a major step toward making that happen. There continues to be debate about terminology, which, however understandable, should not distract from providing the help that individuals need, as Clare Truman describes:

> The way I see it, the PDA critics and the PDA advocates are, in part, arguing for the same thing—that is for children and young people's voices to be heard and respected when they resist and avoid a demand, and for children and young people to be given choice and autonomy over their learning and their lives. (Truman 2021)

It would be helpful if PDA was referred to in future editions of the diagnostic manuals. In the meantime, we can continue to view PDA as an autistic profile. Pediatricians, psychiatrists and psychologists who carry out assessments will hopefully extend how broadly they recognize presentations of autism, and include characteristics that support them to diagnose PDA. There needs to be a broader understanding of autism in America that is not based on an outdated, stereotypical formulation. Autistic individuals can be empathetic, imaginative and communicative, and have positive relationships. We need to have a strength-based lens and move away from focusing on deficits. We all benefit when differences are valued and neurodiversity is appreciated.

It can require courage to shift in parenting approaches from the common advice that has been given for decades. Suggesting time-outs, sticker charts and removing privileges is invariably unhelpful for PDAers. Although we still want to find creative ways to give them rewarding experiences, that is not the same as "working toward a reward," which usually brings too much pressure. Parents need professionals who listen and who understand which approaches are well-suited to their child and why.

The therapeutic community needs to value the in-depth knowledge parents have of their children. Even if parents are unaware of the details of diagnostic categories, they usually know how their child tends to react and have learned what works and what doesn't work for them as a family. They need to be central participants in any interventions involving their child.

Educators and their students will benefit if schools stop equating fair with equal. Meeting everyone's needs does not mean treating them all the same. Students have differing needs whether or not they have an IEP or formal diagnosis. Embracing neurodiversity in our wider communities should include doing so in our schools so that children grow up understanding, accepting and valuing difference. In addition, it seems that there is huge variation of attitudes and requirements across schools, towns, cities and states. Readers need to understand the educational system in the area where they live. Educators need to look underneath the behavior and ask why it is happening, and in doing so they need flexibility, open-mindedness and acceptance. To this end, we have tried to provide a framework to support PDAers at home, at school and in the community that can work with whatever situations children, teens and young adults find themselves in. It is possible for schools, workplaces and communities to provide accommodations to PDA individuals without disregarding the needs of anyone.

All professionals involved will benefit from having a nonjudgmental attitude and a belief in supporting young people to become autonomous. In terms of understanding PDA, it is crucial that they recognize what is underlying PDAers' responses to certain situations or experiences. This needs to incorporate a close eye on wellbeing, self-awareness and providing safe, nurturing environments.

To achieve this, effective support programs should:

- prioritize emotional wellbeing, engagement and creating support networks
- make it a core principle of all involved to understand and value the individual
- collaborate with all partners, keeping the PDAer at the heart of discussions and decisions
- accept the current situation and plan ahead with optimism and high aspirations
- prepare the individual for an autonomous future regarding learning, living arrangements, employment opportunities and relationships.

This book is an opportunity to celebrate the many PDA individuals we know, who are creative, determined, fun, passionate and sociable. We thank you for all you have taught us and for all the great times we have had together. Hopefully this book will also help clinicians, educators and families to feel encouraged and emboldened to engage in constructive discussion about what is possible for PDAers and their networks. It is a goal for PDA North America to provide a unified system of support for parents and to create a

NAVIGATING PDA IN AMERICA

community for PDA children. Let this book be a call to action to spread awareness in your own community. Focusing on today with an eye on tomorrow is a complex and critical challenge, but one that we believe is achievable.

References

American Psychiatric Association (2022) *Diagnostic and Statistical Manual of Mental Disorders: DSM-5-TR.* American Psychiatric Association.

Autism Education Trust (2023) Progression Framework Resource. Available at www.autismeducationtrust.org.uk/resources/progression-framework.

Bateman, B., & Linden, M. A. (2006) *Better IEPs: How to Develop Legally Correct and Educationally Useful Programs.* Verona, WI: IEP Resources, Attainment Co.

Brummer, J., & Thorsborne, M. (2021) *Building a Trauma-Informed Restorative School: Skills and Approaches for Improving Culture and Behavior.* Jessica Kingsley Publishers.

Carpenter, B., Happe, F., & Egerton, J. (eds.) (2019) *Girls and Autism—Educational, Family and Personal Perspectives.* Routledge.

Cat, S. (ed.) (2018) *PDA by PDAers: From Anxiety to Avoidance and Masking to Meltdowns.* Jessica Kingsley Publishers.

Civil Rights Data Collection (2023) 2017–18 State and National Tables. Available at https://civilrightsdata.ed.gov/estimations/2017-2018.

Connolly, S. E., Constable, H. L., & Mullally, S. L. (2023) School distress and the school attendance crisis: A story dominated by neurodivergence and unmet need. *Frontiers in Psychiatry* 14, 1237052.

Csikszentmihalyi, M. (1990) *Flow.* Harper Perennial.

Curtis, S. (2024) *PDA in the Family: Life after the Lightbulb Moments.* Jessica Kingsley Publishers.

Department for Education (2015) *Special Educational Needs and Disability Code of Practice: 0 to 25 Years.* Available at https://assets.publishing.service.gov.uk/media/5a7dcb85ed915d2ac884d995/SEND_Code_of_Practice_January_2015.pdf.

Desautels, L. L. (2020) *Connections over Compliance: Rewiring Our Perceptions of Discipline.* Wyatt-MacKenzie Publishing.

Dundon, R. (2021) *PDA in the Therapy Room: A Clinician's Guide to Working with Children with Pathological Demand Avoidance.* Jessica Kingsley Publishers.

Eaton, J. (2018) *A Guide to Mental Health Issues in Girls and Young Women on the Autism Spectrum: Diagnosis, Intervention and Family Support.* Jessica Kingsley Publishers.

Fidler, R., & Christie, P. (2019) *Collaborative Approaches to Learning for Pupils with PDA: Strategies for Education Professionals.* Jessica Kingsley Publishers.

Fidler, R., & Daunt, J. (2021) *Being Julia: A Personal Account of Living with Pathological Demand Avoidance.* Jessica Kingsley Publishers.

Fisman, S., Wolf, L., Ellison, D., & Freeman, T. (2000) A longitudinal study of siblings of children with chronic disabilities. *Canadian Journal of Psychiatry* 45, 369–375.

Fricker, E. (2022) *The Family Experience of PDA: An Illustrated Guide to Pathological Demand Avoidance.* Jessica Kingsley Publishers.

Gillberg, C., Gillberg, I., Thompson, L., Biskupsto, R., & Billstedt, E. (2015) Extreme (pathological) demand avoidance in autism: A general population study in the Faroe Islands. *European Child and Adolescent Psychiatry* 24, 979–984.

Goleman, D. (1996) *Emotional Intelligence.* Bloomsbury.

Goleman, D. (1998) *Working with Emotional Intelligence.* Bloomsbury.

Gore Langton, E. and Frederickson, N. (2016) Mapping the educational experiences of children with pathological demand avoidance. *Journal of Research in Special Educational Needs* 16(4), 254–263.

Gould, J., and Ashton-Smith, J. (2011) Missed diagnosis or misdiagnosis? Girls and women on the autism spectrum. *Good Autism Practice (GAP)* 12, 34–41.

Greene, R. (2005) *The Explosive Child.* HarperCollins.

Henderson, D., Wayland, S., with White, J. (2023) *Is This Autism? A Guide for Clinicians and Everyone Else.* Routledge.

Holt, J. (1964) *How Children Fail.* Pitman Publishing.

Learning Disabilities Association of America (n.d.) A Parent's Guide to Evaluations, IEPs, and More. Available at https://ldaamerica.org/a-parents-guide-to-evaluations-ieps-and-more/?audience=Parents.

Levine, S., & Ursin, H. (1978) What Is Stress? In Ursin, H., Baade, E., & Levine, S. (eds.) *Psychobiology of Stress.* Academic Press Inc.

Loomes, R., Hull, L., & Mandy, W. P. L. (2017) What is the male-to-female ratio in autism spectrum disorder? A systematic review and meta-analysis. *Journal of the American Academy of Child and Adolescent Psychiatry* 56(6), 466–474.

Lord, C., Rutter, M., & Le Couteur, A. (1994) Autism Diagnostic Interview—Revised: A revised version of a diagnostic interview for caregivers of individuals with possible pervasive developmental disorders. *Journal of Autism and Developmental Disorders* 24, 659–685.

Lord, C., Rutter, M., DiLavore, P. C., Risi, S., Gotham, K., & Bishop, S. (2012) *Autism Diagnostic Observation Schedule, Second Edition (ADOS-2) Manual (Part 1): Modules 1–4.* Western Psychological Services.

Maenner, M. J., Warren, Z., Williams, A. R., Amoakohene, E., et al. (2023) Prevalence and characteristics of autism spectrum disorder among children aged 8 years—Autism and Developmental Disabilities Monitoring Network, 11 Sites, United States, 2020. *MMWR Surveillance Summaries* 72(2), 1–14.

McGillivray, J. A., & Evert, H. T. (2014) Group cognitive behavioral therapy programme shows potential in reducing symptoms of depression and stress among young people with ASD. *Journal of Autism and Developmental Disorders* 44(8), 2041–2051.

Monteiro, M. J., & Stegall, S. (2018) *MIGDAS-2: Monteiro Interview Guidelines for Diagnosing the Autism Spectrum*. Western Psychological Services.

Murphy, L. K. (2020) *Declarative Language Handbook*. Self-published.

Newson, E., Le Maréchal, K., & David, C. (2003) Pathological demand avoidance syndrome: A necessary distinction within the pervasive developmental disorders. *Archives of Diseases in Childhood 88*, 595–600.

O'Nions, E., Gould, J., Christie, P., Gilberg, C., Viding, E., & Happe, F. (2016a) Identifying features of "pathological demand avoidance" using the Diagnostic Interview for Social Communication Disorders (DISCO). *European Child and Adolescent Psychiatry 25*, 407–419.

O'Nions, E., Happe, F., & Viding, E. (2016b) Extreme "pathological" demand avoidance. *DECP Debate British Psychological Society 160*, 18–22.

O'Nions, E., Happe, F., Viding, E., & Noens, I. (2021) Extreme demand avoidance in children with ASD: Refinement of a caregiver report measure. *Advances in Neurodevelopmental Disorders 5*, 269–281.

Osborne, A. G., & Russo, C. J. (2021) *Special Education and the Law: A Guide for Practitioners*. Corwin Press.

PDA Society (2022) *Identifying and Assessing a PDA Profile—Practice Guidelines*. Available at www.pdasociety.org.uk/wp-content/uploads/2023/02/Identifying-Assessing-a-PDA-profile-Practice-Guidance-v1.1.pdf.

PDA Society (2023) How PDA Can Feel. Available at www.pdasociety.org.uk/life-with-pda-menu/how-pda-can-feel.

Petalas, M. A., Hastings, R. P., Nash, S., Lloyd, T., & Dowey, A. (2009) Emotional and behavioural adjustment in siblings of children with intellectual disability with and without autism. *Autism 13*(5), 471–483.

Porges, S. (2017) *The Pocket Guide to the Polyvagal Theory: The Transformative Power of Feeling Safe*. W.W. Norton & Co.

Prizant, B. M. (2019) *Uniquely Human: A Different Way of Seeing Autism*. Souvenir Press.

Raymaker, D. M., Teo, A. R., Steckler, N., Lentz, B., et al. (2020) "Having all of your internal resources exhausted beyond measure and being left with no clean-up crew": Defining autistic burnout. *Autism in Adulthood 2*(2). Available at www.liebertpub.com/doi/10.1089/aut.2019.0079.

Rosenberg, M. (1999) *Nonviolent Communication: A Language of Compassion*. PuddleDancer Press.

Running, A. (2022) *Helping Your Child with PDA Live a Happier Life*. Jessica Kingsley Publishers.

Russell, S. (2018) *Being Misunderstood: Experiences of the Pathological Demand Avoidance Profile of ASD*. PDA Society. Available at www.pdasociety.org.uk/wp-content/uploads/2019/08/BeingMisunderstood.pdf.

Rutter, M., Le Couteur, A., & Lord, C. (2003) *ADI-R: Autism Diagnostic Interview-Revised (ADI-R)*. Western Psychological Services.

Santosh, P. J., Mandy, W. P. L., Puura, K., Kaartinen, M., Warrington, R., & Skuse, D. H. (2009) The construction and validation of a short form of the Developmental, Diagnostic and Dimensional Interview. *European Child and Adolescent Psychiatry 18*(8), 521–524.

Schopler, E., Reichler, R. J., & Rochen Renner, B. (1988) *The Childhood Autism Rating Scale*. Western Psychological Services.

Scott, L., & Westcott, R. (2019) *Can You See Me? Expected to Fit In, Proud to Stand Out*. Scholastic.

Shah, A. (2019) *Catatonia, Shutdown and Breakdown in Autism: A Psycho-Ecological Approach*. Jessica Kingsley Publishers.

Siegel, D. (2020) *The Developing Mind*. Guilford Press.

Skuse, D., Warrington, R., Bishop, D., Chowdhury, U., et al. (2004) The Developmental, Dimensional and Diagnostic Interview (3Di): A novel computerized assessment for autism spectrum disorders. *Journal of the American Academy of Child and Adolescent Psychiatry* 43(5), 548–558.

Stubbe, D. E. (2018) The therapeutic alliance: The fundamental element of psychotherapy. *Focus: The Journal of Lifelong Learning in Psychiatry* 16(4), 402–403.

Toudal, M. (2022) *What Your Autistic Child Wants You to Know: And How You Can Help Them*. Jessica Kingsley Publishers.

Truman, C. (2021) *The Teacher's Introduction to Pathological Demand Avoidance: Essential Strategies for the Classroom*. Jessica Kingsley Publishers.

Wing, L., Leekam, S., Libby, S., Gould, J., & Larcombe, M. (2002) Diagnostic interview for social and communication disorders: Background, inter-rater reliability and clinical use. *Journal of Child Psychology and Psychiatry* 43, 307–325.

Winnicott, D. (1971) *Playing and Reality*. Tavistock Publications.

World Health Organization (2022) *ICD-11: International Classification of Disease*. World Health Organization.

World Health Organization (2023) Health and Well-Being. Available at www.who.int/data/gho/data/major-themes/health-and-well-being.

Wright, P. W. D., & Wright, P. D. (2007) *Wrightslaw: Special Education Law* (2nd edn.). Harbor House Law Press, Inc.

Websites

www.pdasociety.org.uk

https://lizonions.wordpress.com

www.who.int

www.autistica.org.uk

www.kelly-mahler.com

www.asspire.org

https://my.clevelandclinic.org

www.cpsconnection.com

www.kristyforbes.com.au

www.understood.org

https://www2.ed.gov/about/offices/list/ocr/docs/restraint-and-seclusion.pdf

https://hslda.org

https://endseclusion.org

www.autismeducationtrust.org.uk

www.wrightslaw.com

Index